Mastering Products Liability

Mastering Series
Russell Weaver, Series Editor

Mastering Bankruptcy
George W. Kuney

Mastering Civil Procedure
David Charles Hricik

Mastering Criminal Law
Ellen S. Podgor, Peter J. Henning, Neil P. Cohen

Mastering Evidence
Ronald W. Eades

Mastering Legal Analysis and Communications
David Ritchie

Mastering Products Liability
Ronald W. Eades

Mastering Products Liability

Ronald W. Eades
<small>Louis D. Brandeis School of Law
University of Louisville</small>

Carolina Academic Press
Durham, North Carolina

Library of Congress Cataloging in Publication Data

Eades, Ronald W. Mastering products liability / by Ronald W. Eades.

p. cm. —
(Mastering series) Includes index.
ISBN 978-1-59460-423-2 (alk. paper)
ISBN 10: 1-59460-423-1 (alk. paper)
1. Products liability—United States. I. Title. II. Series.
KF1296.E18 2008 346.7303'8—dc22   2008004361

Carolina Academic Press
700 Kent Street
Durham, NC 27701
Telephone (919) 489-7486
Fax (919) 493-5668
www.cap-press.com

Contents

Series Editor's Foreword

The Carolina Academic Press Mastering Series is designed to provide you with a tool that will enable you to easily and efficiently "master" the substance and content of law school courses. Throughout the series, the focus is on quality writing that makes legal concepts understandable. As a result, the series is designed to be easy to read and is not unduly cluttered with footnotes or cites to secondary sources.

In order to facilitate student mastery of topics, the Mastering Series includes a number of pedagogical features designed to improve learning and retention. At the beginning of each chapter, you will find a "Roadmap" that tells you about the chapter and provides you with a sense of the material that you will cover. A "Checkpoint" at the end of each chapter encourages you to stop and review the key concepts, reiterating what you have learned. Throughout the book, key terms are explained and emphasized. Finally, a "Master Checklist" at the end of each book reinforces what you have learned and helps you identify any areas that need review or further study.

We hope that you will enjoy studying with, and learning from, the Mastering Series.

Russell L. Weaver
Professor of Law & Distinguished University Scholar
University of Louisville, Louis D. Brandeis School of Law

Preface

The true beginnings of products liability law can be debated. It may appear to start with Restatement (Second) of Torts § 402A in the 1960s. It could be traced to the abolition of privity for negligence cases in MacPhearson v. Buick in the early 1900s. It could, however, be traced back to Coke on Littleton and the discussion of the fair price doctrine in the 1700s. Whatever the birth date of modern products liability law, it is clear that it had and continues to have a major impact from the mid-20th century until today.

The law developed slowly until the advent of strict liability in tort in the mid-1960's. From that period through the end of the 20th century, the law exploded. Products liability issues were discussed in terms of consumer protection or the harm to manufacturers. Products like automobiles, cigarettes, and prescriptions drugs became the central issues in the debate.

By the end of the 20th century, detractors were seeking to pull back on the extent to which consumers were protected. The Restatement (Third) of Products Liability showed a definite return to negligence. The extent to which that will be followed is still to be seen.

As a topic of study, the above discussion should point out why products liability is exciting. It is a modern development in the law in the United States and worldwide. It has had a major impact on the lives of ordinary people whether they were injured parties who sought relief or employees in factories who felt they lost jobs because companies were unable to compete in that marketplace.

This text is designed to provide a discussion of the broad range of topics that come under the heading of Products Liability. A portion of the history of that area is discussed in order to help illuminate some of the relationships between different areas of the law. The different bases of claims and defenses are also presented. The text tries to provide a discussion of the more common issues that arise in this area. For students taking a course in Products Liability, this work should be useful for most courses in that area. It will provide the basics that will be covered regardless of the specific areas of concern the faculty seeks to provide focus.

At times, this work will need to cite to the Restatement of Torts and the Uniform Commercial Code. The language of those documents is not provided in full, but, instead, attempts are made to explain those materials. It is suggested that the reader of this book should seek out copies of those materials when they are being cited. Being able to read the exact language of the Restatement and the Uniform Commercial Code will assist in the understanding of the material being presented.

Ronald W. Eades
Professor of Law
Louis D. Brandeis School of Law
University of Louisville
Louisville, Kentucky

Mastering Products Liability

Chapter 1

History and Background of Products Liability

History and Background Roadmap

- Understand the early development of the law that created the background for products liability.
- Follow the development of negligence.
- Understand how the development of negligence and warranty led to a doctrine of strict liability in tort.
- Picture how the law will continue to develop in the future.
- Organize the range of theories that make up the bases of liability for product cases.

A. Product?

Products liability is different from many courses studied in law school. Most courses start with a basic area of the law and then work on the bases of liability within that area. Torts, contracts, and property are the best example of that typical format for law school courses. Products liability begins with a type of injury. In products liability, the area of the law is all of the injuries caused by products. Within that area, many topics and issues may arise. There will need to be a little historical material to figure out how the law got to where it is today. The law will also, of course, have to look at possible bases of liability. Products cases, however, use numerous bases of liability. Actions in tort and contract have been and continue to be used for such injuries. It is also necessary to look at the possible plaintiffs and defendants. Due to the complexity of many of the products liability cases, the identity of who can sue and who can be sued is a difficult question. Possible defenses and damages must also be studied. Because of the variety of possible bases of liability and possible plaintiffs and defendants, the nature of the defenses and damages is also varied.

As should be obvious, the material on Products Liability draws from the full spectrum of legal materials. The unifying theme is that all of the injuries were caused by products. It would seem, therefore, that the first issue to be addressed is, "What is a product?" That topic arises throughout the material, but will bear some discussion at this early stage.

A product, that will give rise to a products liability action, is a physical thing. It must be one that could be described as personal property, because the law that is associated with products liability is not concerned with real property. The Uniform Commercial Code, for example, regulates the sale of goods. "Goods" would be the type of items that would be included in products liability actions. Land, real estate, houses, and condominiums, for example, would not be included in a study of products liability actions. Clearly, however, toasters, automobiles, guns, prescription drugs, or machinery of any kind would be considered products.

One of the difficult areas of concern is how to treat services. It would seem that supplying a service would not be considered in the law of products liability. It is clear, however, that some businesses provide a hybrid sales/service. Those businesses might sell products and provide a service. Imagine, for example, a heating contractor that sells a new furnace to a homeowner. The heating contractor then installs the furnace. The sale of the furnace looks like the sale of goods, while the installation looks like a service. The sale should be considered the sale of a product while the installation should be treated as a service. The law concerning those two would be different. Imagine, however, a surgeon that places a heart pacemaker in a patient. In some ways, that looks like the sale of the furnace. The surgeon sold the pacemaker and then installed it. The law might consider the surgeon as selling a product and providing a service. The law, however, will treat the whole transaction by the surgeon as a service. The manufacture of the pacemaker would be the products liability issue. (That will be discussed further in Chapter 6.)

As should be noted, the simple areas of "What is a product?" are easy to see. Some items are clearly products; some activities or items are outside the area of products liability. There are gray areas, however, that will be discussed in detail.

B. Fair Price Doctrine

It is generally assumed by many that consumers have never had much protection by the law. Many assume that consumers were always expected to watch after their own interests with little protection once it was discovered that the item or services purchased were defective. That is not actually the case. Prior to the 1800's, there was a doctrine in the law known as the "Fair Price Doctrine."

The theory behind this doctrine was that if consumers paid a fair price for an item, they should expect to get a fair product in return. The law would enforce this doctrine for those consumers who received less then what was paid.

Some historians believe that such a doctrine would maintain a fair, stable economic system. They also believe that such a doctrine would not encourage growth and development. If everyone was entitled to a fair product for a fair price paid, then there would be no encouragement to speculate. In fact, it would not be possible to engage in the more modern practice of "speculation." The modern stock market, real estate market and commodities market depend, to some extent, on speculation. The seller in those markets believes that the price is either going down or remaining the same in the foreseeable future. The buyer in those markets believes that the price will go up and that the buyer will be able to resell for a profit in the foreseeable future. That is the basis for the modern free market economy. If the law enforced a "Fair Price Doctrine," that could not occur. After the sale, the disappointed party would sue. If the value went up substantially, the seller would claim that a fair price was not paid. If the value went down substantially, the buyer would claim that a fair value was not given for the price paid. Speculative markets would not operate.

Such Fair Price Doctrine, however, was the general rule until sometime in the 1800's. Again, some historians believe the change to "Caveat Emptor" was a method for the law to allow growth and speculation in the free market economy.

C. Caveat Emptor

Caveat Emptor is the doctrine that most people feel has always been the universal theory of transactions in the United States. The phrase, caveat emptor, roughly translates to "let the buyer beware." The theory is that the buyer and seller operate at an arm's length. Each is entitled to price the product and pay for the product at whatever the market will bear. Once the transaction is completed, then there is no recourse. If the value of the product should suddenly increase substantially, then the buyer is entitled to keep the increased value. If the value of the product should suddenly decrease substantially, then the buyer is just left with the bargain that he or she struck. This also applied to defective products. If the buyer purchased a product that ultimately would not or could not perform, then the buyer had no remedy. The buyer was assumed to be on notice to take care of his or her own interest.

It appears that such a rule of law would be highly favorable to sellers. Sellers could sell defective products and enjoy great profits. That would, of course, be true when the product was defective. In times of fluctuating markets and speculative buying, there might be times when buyers of commodities would benefit. If the value of the product purchased escalated rapidly, the buyer would then resell for a huge profit. The originally seller would have no claim.

Several things are worth noting about this period. First, something like "buyer beware" still exists. When a buyer purchases a product that is marked, "as is, with all defects," certain warranties are being disclaimed. Remedies that a buyer might have at law are extinguished. Such phrases are, therefore, much like the old "buyer beware." Second, even during the height of the caveat emptor theory, there were remedies against the truly dishonest seller. Remedies for fraud and intentional misrepresentation of products or goods have a long history. A buyer that had been the victim of such behavior would have some remedy.

It is important to note this combination in the history of the United States of some consumer protection together with some protection of a free and open market. The law in the United States continues to change and grow. It tends to retain elements of consumer protection and protection of the market. At times it may seem to emphasize one over the other, but there are regular returns to a middle ground. In learning the law of products liability, it is useful to see how the law seems to fluctuate between the two polar extremes of protections.

D. Return to Consumer Protection

Although the height of "caveat emptor" was during the 1800's, it probably had a relatively short duration. During the rapid growth of the economy from local to national during and after the industrial revolution and after the Civil War, the law began to recognize some return to consumer protection. It was during the late 1800's that the economy stretched to a national basis as goods moved across the country. The reaching out to consumers by ever more powerful companies, led to some attempt by the law to protect those consumers. The protections would be minor during the early parts of the 1900's and would not reach the strongest point until the 1960's.

The major thrust of the movement to some consumer protection can be seen with the law of privity. The growth of a privity requirement for tort cases and the ultimate abolition of privity for those cases is a central feature of that change.

E. Privity

Privity appears to be a contract issue. When two parties enter into a contract, then the rights and obligations flow between those two parties. Strangers to the contract should have no rights under the contract. Such strangers cannot, for example, sue to enforce the contract. There are some exceptions to that rule, but they are not important here.

Since the issue of privity seems limited to contract, it should not even enter into a discussion of tort remedies. In modern products liability actions, plaintiffs will frequently add claims for breach of warranty. Since warranty claims are in the nature of contract actions, the issue of privity will arise in such claims. That issue is discussed in the material on warranty and proper parties. Tort remedies, however, should not depend on the details of the contract issue of privity.

In the classic case of *Winterbottom v. Wright*, 152 Eng. Rep. 402 (Ex. 1842), the issue of privity got enmeshed in tort. In that case, Wright had agreed to supply and maintain coaches for the Postmaster. Due to a defect in a carriage, one of the drivers, Winterbottom, was injured. When Winterbottom sued Wright for the injuries, the court dismissed the case due to the fact that Winterbottom was not in privity with Wright. The case could have easily been interpreted as a contract case. Wright had a contract to keep the carriages in repair and failed to do anything to honor that commitment. There was clear non-feasance on the part of Wright. There was actually no tort claim for Winterbottom to allege.

Although the case was clearly a contract action and Winterbottom could have no claim due to lack of privity, the court interpreted the decision differently. The courts of the time felt that the case stood for the proposition that privity was required in such cases. There was the concern that the vendors of goods could be held liable to a large number of future, unknown persons without limit. The addition of the privity limit made it possible to restrict such an uncontrollable situation. With that view, privity was thought to be applicable to tort claims.

To a certain extent, this decision in law in the middle 1800's was not a great detriment to the sale and distribution of goods. In that period, many products were purchased directly from the person who made them. In the alternative, even if the seller did not make the goods, the buyer would be relying upon the expertise of the seller in selecting the goods. The typical buyer would be shopping at a general store and purchasing goods that the store owner had selected. It would not be until after the industrial revolution and the Civil War that nation wide sales and distribution began to emerge. It would not be until the early part of the 1900's that buyers would begin to purchase most goods from retailers who had selected goods from a variety of manufacturers. In addition, buyers would begin in the early 1900's to rely more on the name of the manufacturer rather than on the expertise of the retailer.

With the changes in manufacturing, distribution and sales of goods that occurred after *Winterbottom v. Wright*, the early 1900's saw a different type of marketing environment. Manufacturers were producing products and such products were being sold through wholesalers and retailers. There had developed a long marketing chain. With the requirement of privity, modern products liability law could not develop. Privity would restrict any action by an injured plaintiff to claims against the immediate seller. The early 1900's saw a change in the law.

F. Privity Abolished

The privity requirement introduced in *Winterbottom v. Wright* did have exceptions that developed very early. Within a few years of the decision in Winterbottom, courts created the most significant exception for inherently dangerous products. In *Thomas v. Winchester*, 6 N.Y. 397 (1852), the court had to view a case where a bottle of poison had been sold without adequate markings as to its danger. The court found that such a product could cause harm to people and the remote users should have a claim. This type of exception was expanded to allow claims without privity where there was some great danger that could not be easily avoided. Typical examples that fit within this exception were poisons, guns, and explosives.

By the early 1900's, the marketing of products had developed into a modern, national scope. Early automobiles, for example, were assembled in factories from parts made by other component part manufacturers and the final assembler also. Those automobiles were then sold to dealers around the country. Those independent dealers would then sell the automobiles to customers. With that marketing chain, the impact of a privity requirement should be obvious. If a buyer was injured by a defect in the automobile, the only legal recourse would be to sue the local dealership. There could be no action against the final assembler of the component part manufacturer.

In 1916, the Court of Appeals of New York was faced with such a case. In *MacPhearson v. Buick*, 111 N.E. 1050 (N.Y. 1916), MacPhearson had purchased a new Buick from Close Brothers Dealership. One of the wheels on the Buick was defective, collapsed, and caused injury to MacPhearson. The wheel had been manufactured by a component part manufacturer and sold to Buick. MacPhearson sought to sue Buick. The privity requirement would have protected Buick from such claims.

The Court of Appeals in New York reviewed the law in this area and began an expansive view of the exceptions to the privity requirement. Although the court did not specifically abolish the privity requirement, the use of the exceptions in this case would lead to that result. Since earlier courts had not required privity where the product was inherently dangerous, the court opinion worked with that exception. The court found that anything that placed life or limb in danger when negligently made was a thing of danger. As such, privity would not be required. This expansive use of the exception, ultimately led to the complete abolition of the privity rule in negligence actions for defective goods. Subsequently courts found that almost any product negligently made would place life or limb in danger and, therefore, privity should not be required. This became an example where the expansive reading of the exception finally swallowed the rule.

Modern products liability law can probably be traced to the decision in *MacPhearson*. As long as privity remained a requirement, injured plaintiffs could only seek recovery against the immediate seller. If the immediate seller was not subject to suit or no longer in business, the plaintiff had no claim. In addition, manufacturers had little reason to be concerned about litigation. They were virtually exempt from actions by the privity requirement. The ultimate abolition of that requirement opened the whole marketing chain to litigation.

Although the abolition of the privity requirement opened up the whole marketing chain to litigation, claims by plaintiffs were still difficult to win. The claims had to be based on negligence. Negligence required, of course, proof that the defendant failed to use reasonable care in the manufacture or marketing of the product. This would be difficult to prove against those in the marketing chain, and especially against those distant or remote defendants. The law of tort, however, continued to change and the proof problems for plaintiffs were eased.

G. Move from Negligence to Strict Liability

1. Negligence

Negligence was an available remedy for products liability claims from the very creation of negligence liability. A plaintiff injured by a product could sue for damages and recover on proof of the basic claim. The problem with negligence was that the elements of the claim were difficult to prove.

Before the early 1900's, negligence had the difficulty of requiring privity. Injured parties could only sue those with whom they were in privity. As discussed above, privity was abolished in the early 1900's, but the elements of the basic claim remained.

The basic elements of a negligence claim required and still requires that the plaintiff prove the existence of the duty, breach of that duty, an injury and a causal connection between that breach and the injury. The duty was that of a reasonable person of ordinary prudence under similar circumstances. Proving the breach of that duty was and continues to be the most difficult issue.

Proving that the defendant manufacturer or seller failed to use the care and skill of a reasonable person of ordinary prudence under similar circumstances is difficult in any negligence case. It is even more difficult in a products liability case. Although the manufacturer may be held to a higher standard of ordinarily prudent manufacturers, the proof necessary to show the breach is difficult for plaintiff. Since most products liability actions will require proof of the breach of the duty in the manufacturing process, there are two major problems for the plaintiff. The plaintiff must first be able to show what the defendant was doing in the manufacturing process. Where the product is complex and the result of a complex manufacturing process, getting the basic facts of that process may be impossible. Even if the plaintiff can show what the manufacturer did, there will still need to be expert testimony to point out why that was negligent. Experts will clash on what are reasonable manufacturing techniques for complex products. Since plaintiffs have the burden of proof, they will lose more often than not.

The law of torts has found ways to ease the proof problems for plaintiffs. The doctrine of res ipsa loquitur has been used to assist those parties with the burden of proof.

a. Res Ipsa Loquitur

The doctrine of res ipsa loquitur was a court creation that provides assistance in proving the breach of the duty. It traces a history back to an early case dealing with a warehouse and flour barrels. When a flour barrel fell from a window and injured a plaintiff on the street below, an action was brought. Since the plaintiff had the burden of proof, and no way to show how the barrel fell from the window, the plaintiff should have lost the case. The court, however, noted that barrels do not fly from windows in the absence of someone's negligence. Since the defendants had control over the barrel, the defendants should be liable for the harm. The circumstances could be such that the "thing speaks for itself."

That concept became a doctrine that allowed the plaintiff to create an inference that the breach had occurred. The use of the inference would allow the plaintiff to get the case to a jury. As noted above, the doctrine of res ipsa loquitur has two basic elements. It is necessary for the plaintiff to prove that:

1. The instrumentality of the injury was in the exclusive custody or control of the defendant; and
2. The event that occurred is one that would not normally occur in the absence of negligence.

It should be obvious that this doctrine is of great assistance to plaintiffs in many negligence cases. It should also be obvious that it would rarely be of assistance in a products liability case. A product is normally made by a manufacturer, sold through wholesalers and then through retailers. By the time the plaintiff gets possession of the product, that product has been in the hands of several people. By the time the accident or injury occurs, there would be even more people who had contact with the product. Being able to prove the element of exclusive custody or control would be virtually impossible.

b. Proof without Fault

The difficulty with res ipsa loquitur was best illustrated in an exploding soft drink bottle. Throughout most of the 1900's, soft drinks were sold in returnable bottles. They would be sold and a deposit would be paid on the bottle. When the bottle was returned, the purchaser would get a return of the deposit. The bottle would then be returned to the bottling plant. The bottling plant would clean, sterilize, and then refill the bottle. Once refilled, the bottle would be resold. These returnable bottles had the problem of creating some products liability issues. They might be found to have some type of foreign substance in them or the bottle might explode.

In the landmark case of *Escola v. Coca Cola Bottling Co*, 150 P.2d 436 (Cal. 1944), a soft drink bottle exploded and caused injury. The bottle was one of the returnable bottles. It had been filled and then delivered to a restaurant for sale and consumption there. It had been delivered to the stock room of that establishment and not used until the following day. When someone went into the stock room to pick up some soft drinks, the bottle exploded. The injured party sued the bottling company.

The Supreme Court of California allowed the plaintiff to use the doctrine of res ipsa loquitur. The court reasoned that soft drink bottles could only explode for one of three reasons. The bottles would have to have been negligently manufactured in the first instance, negligently over-pressurized during the refilling process, or damaged due to negligent handling. Since of those options assume some type of negligence, then res ipsa was appropriate. The problem, of course, was that the bottle had been out of the hands of the bottling company for over a day. Proving exclusive custody or control in the hands of the defendant was impossible. The court majority opinion, however, thought it was sufficient that the plaintiff could prove that it was unlikely that anyone else had tampered with the bottle.

Justice Roger Traynor of the California Supreme Court agreed with the outcome of the decision, but offered a different explanation for his reasoning. He felt that using res ipsa loquitur was incorrect. The actually elements of that doctrine were not met in the case. He offered the idea that manufactures who place items on the market, knowing that the items will be used without inspection, should be liable when those items are defective and cause harm. In short, Justice Traynor was inviting the courts in California to adopt strict liability in tort for product injuries.

A close review of the case illustrates how the doctrine of strict liability in tort may grow naturally out of the doctrine of negligence. Negligence does require proof that the defendant failed to use reasonable care. There is this well known requirement of fault. The doctrine of res ipsa loquitur, however, removes the most difficult fault element from the plaintiff's burden of proof. By allowing the plaintiff to infer the breach, the law is using something like strict liability. The plaintiff must only prove duty, injury and a causal connection between the duty and injury. Any proof of fault based conduct will have to come from the defendant in terms of proving absence of breach of reasonable care. Justice Traynor's concurring opinion merely pointed out the very short step from negligence, with the use of res ipsa loquitur, to a doctrine of strict liability. His opinion also suggested that courts were actually applying a doctrine of strict liability, but hiding it under a broad use of res ipsa loquitur. It would be another 20 years before Justice Traynor could convince the rest of the California Supreme Court to adopt his theory. That history is discussed below.

2. Warranty

While the negligence theory in tort was slowly changing to provide an easier method of recovery for injured plaintiffs, the law of contracts was also moving in that direction. The law of warranty in contract was creating rights for those consumers.

Warranty law developed in contract and carried along with it many of the basic contract requirements. These requirements would include privity of contract and notice of breach before recovery. Privity and notice were logical additions to the traditional commercial contract setting, but provided limitations in the area of consumer goods.

For most contract remedies, privity is an obvious requirement. When two parties agree to terms of a contract, third parties should not be able to take advantage of those terms. There are, of course, some well known contract exceptions to the privity rule for third party beneficiary contracts, but those are limited. When two parties agree to terms, those two parties have the right to exclude others from the agreement. Just because party "A" would like to offer party "B" a warranty or guarantee does not mean that party "A" would like to

offer that warranty or guarantee to the world. In the consumer goods transaction, however, difficulties arose. If a manufacturer of a product made certain warranties to a retailer, but it was an ultimate purchaser that was injured,
the question arose as to whether the ultimate purchaser should be able to see
relief for that warranty from the manufacturer. As courts began to break down
the privity requirement and allow that recovery back up the chain of distribution, the remedy began to look more like tort than contract.

The requirement of notice before a remedy could be sought also made sense
in the commercial setting. If two large commercial companies had done business for a long period of time, a constant flow of information between the two
would also continue. If a product was defective, the purchaser would naturally contact the manufacturer. In the consumer transaction, however, that
might not happen. A consumer would probably have purchased the product
from a retailer. If the product injured the consumer, that consumer might contact the retailer, but would probably not think to contact the manufacturer. If
giving notice was required, the manufacturer could escape responsibility for the
harm. Again, as courts began to reduce the requirement for giving notice, the
claims in warranty began to look more like tort remedies.

By the middle 20th century, courts had begun to reduce reliance on privity
and notice rules before allow consumers to recover under warranties. Where
a manufacturer had made warranties or even where the law had created implied
warranties, the courts were allowing the consumer to use these claims. Since
warranties were originally contract remedies, they have always been in the nature of strict liability. There is no requirement of proof of fault before recovering in warranty. Plaintiffs just have to prove that the product does not meet
the warranty.

3. Strict Liability

When students first read of strict liability in tort for product injuries, it appears to be something that arose suddenly and unexpected. The case of *Greenman v. Yuba Power Products, Inc.*, 59 Cal. 2d 57, 27 Cal. Rptr. 679, 377 P.2d
897 (1963) appears to have arisen without precedence. A causal reading of the
Restatement (Second) of Torts § 402A (1964) also appears unexpected. The
above noted history should begin to dispel the myth that strict liability was
unexpected. It was the natural progression of, at least, 50 years of development. The movement in negligence and warranty law would have predicted
the emergence of strict liability in tort.

The *Greenman* case was a good vehicle to move negligence and warranty
claims to strict liability in tort. The plaintiff had gotten a wood working tool

as a gift and was using it. A piece of wood flew off the tool and struck him. He was injured and wanted to sue the manufacturer and seller of the tool. The claim would be based on negligence and warranty. Negligence, of course, would have been difficult to prove because of the requirement of showing the failure of the defendants to use reasonable care. The warranty claims would have been difficult because the plaintiff did not give notice to the defendants of the claim for an extended period of time. The case reached the Supreme Court of California and Justice Traynor wrote the opinion. It is worth noting that Justice Traynor had written the concurring opinion in the earlier case of *Escola v. Coca Cola Bottling Co*, 150 P.2d 436 (Cal. 1944). That was, of course, the negligence case where Justice Traynor had suggested the idea of strict liability in tort. In the *Greenman* opinion, Justice Traynor was able to get a majority of the Supreme Court of California to agree with his position. The opinion expressed the idea that the recovery by a plaintiff for injuries due to a product defect should not depend on the details of warranty law. It should be based in tort. The defendant should be responsible for injuries when a product is sold which has a defect and causes injury.

During the late 1950's and the early 1960's, the American Law Institute had been working on a draft of the Restatement (Second) of Torts. Language which suggested strict liability in tort had been debated by the drafters and members of the American Institute. In 1964, the American Law Institute published Restatement (Second) of Torts § 402A. This section provided that a seller of products could be liable for physical harm to persons or property caused by a product sold by that defendant if that product was in a defective condition unreasonably dangerous. (The full details of strict liability in tort will be discussed in the chapter on that specific topic.)

Comparing strict liability to negligence and the implied warranties, the similarities may be seen. As compared to negligence, strict liability in tort is a tort claim. It allows recovery for personal injury and property damage by a foreseeable plaintiff. Strict liability, however, does not require proof that the defendant was "at fault." Proof concerning condition of the product and not defendant's conduct is the critical issue. As compared to the implied warranties, strict liability in tort does not require proof of fault. Just like the implied warranties, the condition of the product is the issue in dispute. Unlike the implied warranties, however, strict liability in tort does not require notice or privity.

Change is law usually proceeds at a slow pace. It is rare for a state law issue to be adopted in one state and then immediately be adopted in others. The speed at which strict liability in tort was adopted across the United States was unprecedented. Within 10 years of the publication of Restatement (Second) of Torts § 402A, the vast majority of states had adopted it. It would be the major issue for discussion in tort law over the next 40 years.

4. Misrepresentation

Misrepresentation is a claim for relief in tort that, at times, also bears similarity to one of the warranty claims. Misrepresentation appears to be a claim that is similar to express warranty. Misrepresentation has been used for product injuries for an extended time, but received some changes with the publication of the Restatement (Second) of Torts.

Misrepresentations for product injuries are the same as any other misrepresentation. The details of that claim will be discussed in the chapter devoted to that topic but a few comments can be made. The claim requires that the plaintiff prove that the defendant made a false representation of material fact, that the defendant intended for the plaintiff to rely upon the statement, that the plaintiff justifiably rely upon the statement and that the plaintiff suffered damages as a result of that reliance.

Prior to the Restatement (Second) of Torts, it was also necessary to prove either negligence or intent on the part of the defendant. For negligence the plaintiff would have to prove that the defendant failed to use reasonable care to determine whether the statement was true or false. For intent the plaintiff would have to prove that the defendant knew the statement was false or spoke in reckless disregard of the truth or falsity of the statement.

The Restatement (Second) of Torts added a form of strict liability for misrepresentation when it concerned a product. Restatement (Second) of Torts § 402B allowed for recovery for innocent misrepresentations concerning a product when the other elements were met. This addition of strict liability misrepresentation claims meant that a plaintiff could sue for misrepresentation and the basis of the conduct of the defendant was not important.

In comparing misrepresentation to express warranty, therefore, some similarities can be seen. Both require a false representation of a material fact and both require reliance or something like it. Misrepresentation, however, is a tort and does not depend on some of the problems associated with warranty. A claim in misrepresentation does not require notice

H. Multiple Bases of Liability Allowed

The preceding parts of this chapter have discussed the different types of claims that may be used for injuries that result from products and the historical background that produced them. Throughout the discussion it has been mentioned that some of those claims may use different bases of liability. It is important to note a few particular items about bases of liability before going further.

There are three and only three bases of liability in law. All legal actions, whether they are civil or criminal, will use one of those three bases of liability. Those three bases of liability are (1) intent, (2) negligence, and (3) strict liability. Those three bases are usually discussed in detail in a first year course in torts, but they also can been seen as applying to all other types of claims.

In criminal law, for example, most crimes are seen as intentional crimes. There is usually an element of intent. That intent may be expressed as a need for proving the mental state or "mens rea." There are some crimes that allow the prosecution to succeed by proving negligence. Negligent homicide is one such example. Strict liability crimes are virtually nonexistent. Something like receiving a ticket for "over time parking" may be viewed as a strict liability crime.

Contract actions are usually strict liability. A breach of contract is actionable without proof of fault. If a seller fails to deliver the goods, the seller is liable for the loss. If a buyer fails to pay for the goods, the buyer is liable. If the parties want there to be some form of fault or excuse of performance, it may be written into the contract. There are times, for example, that major commercial contracts will have clauses that excuse performance for acts of God or labor disputes. Unless the excuse is written into the contract, the action is one in strict liability.

Since warranty claims are actually a form of contract claim, warranty claims are based on strict liability. This is true even when the action is one that is using warranty for damages resulting from product injuries. There is no need to prove some fault on the part of the defendant's conduct. The plaintiff does not have to prove that the defendant intended to breach the warranty or failed to use reasonable care to comply with the warranty. Proving the breach of the warranty is sufficient.

Tort claims can, of course, be based on intent, negligence and strict liability. That simple statement carries over into actions based on tort when the cause of the injury was a product defect. If, for example, the seller intentionally or recklessly makes a defective product, or sells a product knowing that it can cause harm, the claim in tort is for intent. Although this may seem unnecessary since strict liability is available, the awardable damages are different. If the plaintiff can prove the intent, recovery for punitive damages will be allowed. In addition to intent, a claim for a product injury may also be based on negligence. This would require that the plaintiff prove that the defendant failed to use reasonable care in the manufacture or sale of the product. Finally, after the Restatement (Second) of Torts § 402A, a plaintiff may also recover for product injuries using strict liability.

At this point, it may appear somewhat confusing. Plaintiffs may sue using warranty, misrepresentation and tort. Those claims, depending on the facts, circumstances and law, may be based on intent, negligence or strict liability. In fact, most plaintiffs' lawyers will use all of that when they have a big products liability claim. The lawyer will assume that the initial complaint should raise all of those issues and allow the parties to work through the details as they go through discovery and trial. Again, the details of each of those types of claims and their appropriate basis of liability will be discussed in the specific chapter on those topics.

I. Types of Defect

In the above material, the idea that a product must be defective has been assumed. Actions for strict liability require that the product be defective. It is important to note that there are three possible ways that a product may be defective. Products may be defective due to design, manufacturing, or a failure to warn. (Each of these is more fully discussed, together with discussions of proof problems, in chapters specifically dealing with these issues.)

Manufacturing defects may be some of the easiest to prove. These occur when the product is different than it was intended to be by the manufacturer. The specific product that injured the plaintiff is different then the rest of that particular product line. Typically it may have been the result of some error made during the manufacturing process. It should be obvious that one of the reactions to such cases is to require manufacturers to use greater quality assurance in the manufacture of their products.

Design defects may be some of the most difficult to prove. The specific product that injured the plaintiff is manufactured exactly as designed and intended by the defendant. The plaintiff, however, will have to allege and prove that the design of the product was flawed and that it could have been designed in a better fashion. Typically, the plaintiff will have to prove that different and feasible alternative design was available for the product. If a plaintiff wins such a case, it puts a hardship on the manufacturer. A court determination of a design defect will mean that the whole product line is defective. The manufacturer may have to completely redesign the product and begin making them differently. In addition, those that have already been sold may create future lawsuits.

Failure to warn cases have a series of their own special problems. With such cases, the product is usually manufactured correctly and there is no better design. The plaintiff is alleging that the product has some risks associated with its use and that the defendant needed to warn the plaintiff of those risk. Although it appears possible to require the mere addition of a better warning to the product, that brings its own problems. Some products are so covered with warnings that consumers don't read any of the warnings.

In filing litigation, attorneys for the plaintiffs will frequently claim more than one possible type of defect. Although the action may be primarily based on manufacturing or design defects, it is common for the plaintiff to add a claim for failure to warn to all of them.

J. Restatement (Third) of Products Liability and Back to Negligence

The Restatement (Second) of Torts was published in 1964. The adoption of strict liability was rapid. Within 10 years, a vast majority of the states had adopted Restatement (Second) of Torts § 402A. The reaction against those adoptions and the criticism of strict liability was also rapid in coming. Text writers and some courts complained about the use and application of that doctrine.

The primary complaint was that strict liability did not work well for design cases and failure to warn cases. It was recognized that strict liability worked well for manufacturing cases. When a product was sold in a condition that was different than it was designed to be in, the courts had no trouble finding liability. Relieving the plaintiff of the requirement of proving fault also seemed appropriate. Proof could be simply that the individual product was different, the difference created a serious risk, and that defect caused an injury.

Design cases proved harder to decide. Juries would have to decide that something about the design made the product unreasonably dangerous. The difficulty was that most products have some danger associated with the design. That should not give rise to liability. Manufacturers were not intended to be the insurer of the safety of the product. A good example of the difficulty could be the common kitchen butcher knife. Butcher knives are designed to be sharp. The knife must be able to cut up meat, fruit and vegetables. That also means that it will cut the user's hand. There does not appear to be a way to design such a butcher knife that will cut meat but will not cut the user's hand. If a purchaser of the butcher knife cuts his or her own hand with it while trying to chop up some carrots, there should not be liability for the harm. Of course, if the blade snapped in half during the chopping due to the selection of low quality metal in the design of the knife and that snapped off blade flew up and cut the plaintiff, then the manufacturer should be liable. Courts were faced with the difficulty of trying to fashion a test that could be explained to a jury that would allow them to make those types of distinctions when faced with a claim.

Additional problems with design defects could arise because every design of a product is a compromise. Automobiles provide a good example. Safe automobiles would be large, strong and heavy. Fuel efficient automobiles would be light and small. Automobile designers must balance those conflicting concerns. That decision making appeared to some to be more of a "reasonable care" choice then a strict liability issue.

Failure to warn cases also created difficulties with strict liability. There was some initial impulse to hold defendants liable when they failed to warn of risks associate with the product even if the defendant did not know of the risk. In fact, it could have been suggested that the defendant should be liable for failure to warn even when the risk was unknowable by anyone. That was seen as making the manufacturer something of an insurer of the safety of the user of the product. Early failure to warn cases began to require the warning when the defendant knew or should have known of the risk. That test, of course, looks like negligence.

When the American Law Institute began to propose and ultimately adopt the Restatement (Third) of Products Liability in the 1990's, changes occurred. Although manufacturing cases still look like strict liability, design and warning cases show some return to negligence. Those topics will be further discussed in later chapters. It is important to note that jurisdictions are just starting to review products liability cases in light of this new restatement. Only the future will tell whether the suggestions in the Restatement (Third) will be adopted.

K. Federal Involvement

One final note about the future must be considered. Tort law and warranty law has long been considered an area for state law development. Because of the pressures brought to bear by product liability litigation, reductions in the opportunity for plaintiff actions have been sought at all levels. The Federal Government, through federal legislation and federal court action, has entered the area of products liability law. Some of those examples are discussed in later chapters. If states do not move to reduce claims by plaintiffs, there will probably be continuing federal action in this area.

History and Background Checkpoints

- Modern products liability law did not arise suddenly in the middle of the 20th century. The trends seen over the last few years are a result of several hundred years of law development.

- Negligence was the earliest form of modern products liability. The move away from privity as a requirement made it possible to open up the chain of distribution to actions by injured consumers.

- By eliminating the difficult proof problems with negligence and warranty, a doctrine of strict liability in tort emerges.

- Modern product liability cases may use negligence, strict liability and even intent as bases of claims. Those bases may be used in both tort and warranty allegation.

- The future of products liability may continue to change. As states review the Restatement (Third) of Torts the role of strict liability may be diminished.

Chapter 2

Negligence

Negligence Roadmap
- Understand the basic elements of negligence law.
- Be able to apply res ipsa loquitur to a products liability case.
- Determine the recoverable damages in a negligence claim.

A. Elements

Negligence is a standard basis of liability in tort law. As such, it can, of course, be used when a product causes an injury. The law of negligence, as applied in a products liability claim, is governed by the usual negligence rules that were discussed in a first year course in torts. The major difference is that the instrumentality that caused the injury was a product.

A discussed earlier, the major problem with negligence generally in the late 1800's was the existence of a privity requirement. When plaintiffs were injured by a product, they could only sue those parties with whom they were in privity. As modern manufacturing and distribution chains began to develop, this rule limited the use of negligence.

In the early 1900's, the case of *MacPhearson v. Buick*, 111 N.E. 1050 (N.Y. 1916), marked a change in the law. That case was interpreted to abolish the privity requirement in negligence. Plaintiffs could be free to sue and recover from other defendants that were in the chain of distribution. This could, of course, include manufacturers, wholesalers and the retailers. At this point in the development of the law, the use of negligence became one of the primary tools with which to litigate products liability cases. The use of negligence continues today.

To use the negligence claim it is important to understand the basic elements. The elements may be stated as:

1. The existence of a duty;
2. A breach of that duty;
3. Injury by the plaintiff; and

4. A causal connection between the breach of the duty and the injury.

Each of those must be understood. (For a lesson on negligence, see CALI Lessons, Negligence, http://www2.cali.org)

In many negligence cases outside of the products liability area, the question of whether a duty arose is a difficult problem. In products liability cases, the problem is somewhat simplified. The manufacture and sale of a product is held to create a duty to the purchaser, users, and those who may be ultimately injured by the product. The creation of the duty is, therefore, not a problem in products liability case. Manufacturers, wholesalers, retailers and others in the chain of distribution are held to have a duty to parties injured by the product.

Once it is determined that there is a duty, the question arises as to what is that duty. As with other negligence cases, the courts usually say that the duty is to use the care and skill of a reasonable person of ordinary prudence under similar circumstances. There may be some variation on this rule. Manufacturers of products appear to be experts in their field. Because of that status, courts may use something approaching an expert standard of negligence. Rather than considering the manufacturer merely as a reasonable person of ordinary prudence, the courts can consider the expert as one having greater knowledge of how the product should be designed, manufactured and produced. This step alone would then suggest that expert testimony concerning what other similar manufacturers would do may be necessary to illuminate the appropriate standard.

The standard of care may also be changed by other circumstances. As with other typical negligence cases, the existence of professional standards, legislation, or other codes may set a standard different from the reasonable care standard.

Product design is frequently the subject of state or federal regulation. Complex products such as automobiles or airplanes are usually highly regulated. The failure to comply with such regulations would fit the negligence per se formulae. Courts would use the regulation or code as the standard of care for the design of the product. The failure to meet that regulation would be the breach of the duty. Of course, meeting or exceeding the regulation is not an automatic defense to an action. Courts can still determine that regulations or industry standards are too low.

The duty for sellers of products, therefore, may be stated in several ways. Some courts may state it simply as the duty to use reasonable care. Others may elevate it to the standard of similar professionals. In special cases, applicable industry standards or regulations may set the standard. Once the duty of care is articulated, it becomes a jury question as to whether that duty has been breached. The breach of the duty is more fully discussed in the next section on Failure to Use Reasonable Care.

As with all negligence cases, the plaintiff must have suffered an injury in order to recover for negligence. The injury can be any physical injury in the nature of personal injury or property damage. The typical products liability will have both personal injury and property damage. The plaintiff, or some user of the product, may suffer severe personal injury when a product fails. Everything from automobile accidents to burning appliances may cause the plaintiff to suffer those personal injuries. In addition, property damage may result from product failures. An appliance that catches on fire may also burn down a person's home. That additional property damage would be recoverable. As should be obvious, it is rarely difficult to prove the element of injury in a products liability case.

It is important to remember, however, that pure economic losses are not recoverable in negligence. If the plaintiff suffered some lost of profits from a business or even reduced value of the product itself that would not be recoverable under this type of claim. The plaintiff would need to add a claim for breach of warranty.

Causation is also required for negligence. Proof of causation must address both cause in fact and proximate case. Although causation may, at times, be a problem, many products liability cases are clear on this area. When a product fails, it is usually easy to show that the failure caused the injury. When an appliance catches on fire, the destruction of the rest of the house seems to flow naturally from that defect. There are times, however, when proof of causation is difficult. When a serious accident occurs, it may be hard to determine the exact cause of the original accident. When, for example, an automobile accident occurs, there may be substantial damage done to the automobile. The plaintiff may point to some of those defects in the auto and claim that those defects caused the accident. The defendants may claim that the automobile was in perfect shape until it was wrecked through driver error. All of the defects that are now seen in the automobile were caused by the accident. It is clear that the use of expert testimony is frequently required on the causation element in products liability cases.

B. Failure to Use Reasonable Care

Proving the breach of the duty is usually the most difficult part of a products liability case brought in negligence. As noted above, the usual duty is that of a reasonable person of ordinary prudence. Courts will usually expand that to a defendant who is in the business of manufacturing or selling the type of product in question. That standard hold the defendant to something like the duty of a professional.

Even though the defendant is held to that high standard, proving the breach of that duty is difficult. The first difficulty is just having the available evidence. Since the proof will require showing what a reasonable manufacturer, wholesaler or retailer would have done, expert testimony is required.

Even having expert testimony for the plaintiff may not be sufficient to be successful in the case. When the plaintiff seeks to prove that the manufacturer was negligent, there must be proof of what reasonable care would have been and what the manufacturer actually did. Being able to discover the exact conduct that was unreasonable may be difficult. If the unreasonable conduct occurred within a factory, the manufacturer may not know what happened. Plaintiffs' experts may be forced to speculate as to the nature of the conduct.

Proving the wholesalers and retailers were negligent is even more difficult. Wholesalers and retailers merely sell products that are already prepared. Courts have been unwilling to find that a reasonable wholesaler or retailer would have inspected a product. Imagine, for example, that a plaintiff suffers an injury because there are small pebbles in a can of peas. That can of peas should have been shipped to a grocery wholesaler in a large cardboard box together with 24 to 48 other cans of peas. No reasonable wholesaler would open the box to inspect the cans. Wholesaler merely ship the boxes on to grocery retailers. Once the grocery retailer receives the box, the grocer will merely open the box and put the cans of peas on the shelf. No grocer would open the cans of peas to inspect for pebbles. The evidence would show, therefore, that the wholesaler and retailer acted reasonably.

Proving negligence against wholesalers and retailers is virtually impossible. About the only duty that a plaintiff can allege is some duty to inspect the product for defects. Courts have been unwilling to impose a duty to inspect on such defendants.

It is obvious, therefore, that plaintiffs have a difficult time being successful in negligence for a products liability case. Proving breach of the duty is the most difficult part of that claim. There are some cases, however, that give the plaintiffs some assistance with proving that element.

C. Res Ipsa Loquitur

Res ipsa loquitur is a well known tort doctrine that assists the plaintiff with proving the element of breach of the duty. Roughly translated, "Res ipsa loquitur" means that the thing speaks for itself. The doctrine is used where the plaintiff does not have clear proof of the breach of the duty, but there is an inference created that the breach of the duty probably occurred. In order to use res ipsa loquitur to help prove the breach, the plaintiff must offer evidence of two elements. The plaintiff must show that (1) the instrumentality of the injury was in the exclusive custody or control of the defendant, and (2) that the type of accident that occurred does not normally occur in the absence of negligence. (For a lesson on res ipsa loquitur, see CALI Lessons, Res Ipsa Loquitur, http://www2.cali.org)

If the plaintiff can offer evidence of the elements of res ipsa loquitur, most jurisdictions will treat the doctrine as an inference. This will, at least, allow the plaintiff to get the element of breach of the duty to the jury and leave it up to the jury to determine whether the breach has been proven. Without this evidence, plaintiffs would lose most negligence cases in products liability by a directed verdict.

The doctrine of res ipsa loquitur assists with some negligence cases, but not all. The element that requires that the type of accident be one that does not normally occur in the absence of negligence is usually not the problem. Automobile axles do not break; appliances do not catch on fire; and peas do not contain pebbles unless there is negligence somewhere. That alone does not solve the plaintiffs' problems.

With the wholesalers and retailers, the courts rarely even get that far. As noted above, such defendants do not have a duty to inspect. Res ipsa loquitur merely helps prove breach of the duty it does not create a duty. If there is no duty, then res ipsa loquitur is of no assistance.

For the manufacturer, proving that the manufacturer had the exclusive custody or control of the product is difficult. Automobiles and appliances, for example, would normally have been used and maintained by the plaintiff or others for some time after those products left the hands of the defendant. Exclusive custody or control would be hard to prove. Even the can of peas may have traveled through several hands while being picked, cleaned, and processed before canning. At least with the peas, the manufacturer may have been responsible for the cleaning, processing and canning. If so, the manufacturer would be held to have breached a duty.

Although res ipsa loquitur appears to be a useful doctrine for plaintiff and it is one that plaintiffs use in negligent products liability cases, it does not always lead to success. The absence of a duty on the part of some defendants and the difficulty with proving the elements of res ipsa loquitur means that many negligent products liability cases are decided as defendant's verdicts.

D. Other Problem Areas with Negligence

Even if the plaintiff is able to prove the duty and the breach of the duty in a negligence products liability case, there are several additional problem areas for plaintiffs. The broad issue of proximate cause and the more narrow issues of damages raise particular problems in negligence.

Causation, as in all negligence cases, remains a problem in products liability. The plaintiff must prove both cause in fact and proximate cause.

Cause in fact is ordinarily proven by the "but for" test. The plaintiff must prove that the accident would not have occurred "but for" the negligence of the defendant. Where there is only one likely cause of the event, the test appears to work well. In products liability cases, however, there are frequently multiple causes. Where, for example, there is the claim that a drug caused a serious injury or complication; there may be multiple possible explanations for the injury. The drug may be only one of those explanations. The courts have begun to use a "substantial factor" analysis for this type of case. In order for the plaintiff to be successful, it is not necessary to prove that the product was the one, sole cause of the injury. It is only necessary to prove that the negligence was a substantial factor in bringing about the injury.

Proximate cause is also a recurring problem in negligence. As in most negligence cases, jurisdictions use a variety of tests for proximate cause. One good explanation and common used test is that the injury must have been the natural and probable cause of the injury. This has been expanded to mean, in some jurisdictions, that the injury must have been foreseeable to the reasonable person. Frequently, this proof is not that difficult. It is usually obvious that if a product is negligently made, it will cause serious injury.

One additional problem with proximate cause is the issue of the foreseeable plaintiff. Since the abolition of privity for negligence, the law has needed a test that would limit liability to some group of people. The courts have been unwilling to expand negligence liability to all possible plaintiffs. The test has been that the defendant is liable to foreseeable plaintiffs. For the negligent products liability case, some examples can be seen. Obviously, the purchaser of the product will be seen as a foreseeable plaintiff. In addition, other users are typically seen as foreseeable plaintiffs. A more difficult issue may arise with what might be called passive users or bystanders. When an automobile is defective, it is pretty obvious that it may hurt the driver and passengers. It may also hurt passengers in other cars involved in an accident. When the automobile leaves the roadway and hits a pedestrian walking along the street, the defendant manufacturer may claim that the plaintiff-pedestrian was unforeseeable. Courts have been inclined to extend the reach of foreseeable plaintiff to a broad group. Such injured parties, for example, would probably be held to be foreseeable plaintiffs.

The final problem of damages in a negligent products liability action should be addressed. As noted earlier, plaintiffs in such actions can recover for personal injury and property damage. That would include a plaintiffs own personal injury. The personal injury may include medical bills, pain and suffering and lost wages. The plaintiff could also recover for damage to property that the negligently made product caused. Where an appliance burns down a house, the plaintiff could probably recover for the house.

Pure economic losses are not recoverable in tort. This would mean that a plaintiff could not recover in negligence or strict liability for those pure economic losses. An easy example of such losses may be seen. If a plaintiff purchased a truck to use in a business, the loss of profits in the business due to the malfunction of the truck would be a pure economic loss. A harder question arises, however, when the product damaged in such a way as to not be worth as much as it should have been. Where, for example, the truck is wrecked, that appears to be a property damage case. Courts routinely hold, however, that the loss of value, even due to damage, of the product itself is an economic loss and not property damage. If the plaintiff wants to recover for that loss, a warranty claim would be necessary.

Negligence Checkpoints

- Negligence requires proof of
  1. duty;
  2. breach of duty;
  3. injury on the part of the plaintiff; and
  4. a causal connection between the breach and the injury.

- Res ipsa loquitur is available in negligent products liability cases if the plaintiff can prove that
  1. the instrumentality of the injury was in the exclusive custody or control of the defendant; and
  2. the type of accident that occurred does not normally occur in the absence of negligence.

- Plaintiffs can recover personal injury and property damages in a negligent products liability action. Pure economic losses are not recoverable.

Chapter 3

Strict Liability in Tort

Strict Liability Roadmap

- Learn the basic elements of Restatement (Second) of Torts § 402A.

- Understand the application of the various tests for "defective condition unreasonably dangerous."

A. Basic Elements of Restatement (Second) of Torts 402A

1. Introduction

The major change in the law of torts in the second half of the 20th century was the adoption of strict liability in torts for injuries caused by products. As noted in some of the historical materials discussed in the earlier chapters, this process took a long period of time and development in several areas of the law. It also took the combination of court decisions and work by the American Law Institution. It was, however, the work of the American Law Institute in the Restatement (Second) of Torts that put strict liability in tort in a format that courts across the country felt comfortable adopting. Within 10 years of the publication of the Restatement (Second) of Torts, a vast majority of the state jurisdictions had adopted the strict liability. The basic format of strict liability for product injuries can, therefore, be learned by studying the terms expressed by the American Law Institute in Restatement (Second) of Torts § 402A.

The Restatement (Second) of Torts § 402A has a list of elements. Even after adopting the section, state courts have had to spend considerable time working through the details of those elements. Some of the elements have not caused major difficulties. Other elements have been the cause of numerous appellate decisions. It is necessary to understand each of the elements of strict liability for product injuries.

2. Business Seller

The Restatement speaks of one in the business of selling the product. Strict liability for product injuries is intended to force the cost of injuries to be born by those most able to bear that cost. It is assumed that the cost of injuries ought to be one of the costs of doing business. When a manufacturer sells a defective product that causes substantial harm to consumers, that manufacturer ought to pay that cost. That cost should not be shifted over to the injured consumer to pay.

In addition to the injury cost being a cost of doing business, it is assumed that the defendant should have some authority to work back up the chain of distribution in order to make sure that future products are less dangerous. When a manufacturer, for example, is forced to pay for the costs of injuries due to one of its products, that manufacturer will be encouraged to seek to make a better product.

In short, the theory of strict liability for product injuries is based on at least two hopeful theories. The defendant paying the cost of injuries is best able to bear that cost as a cost of doing business, and that same defendant is best able to work to bring about a safer product. In order to accomplish these goals, it is necessary to limit the strict liability to those "in the business" of selling the product.

Easy examples of the appropriate defendant may be seen. Obviously, manufacturers, wholesalers, and retailers fit the category of business sellers. They are in the chain of distribution of the product. They can consider the cost of injuries that their products cause as a cost of doing business. They may also be able to work back up the chain of distribution in order to encourage the manufacturer to make a safer product.

Examples of those not within the category of those in the business of selling the product may also be easily seen. When a person has a yard sale and sells an old toaster or blender that he or she wants to get rid of, that person is not in the business of selling small appliances. That person is not able to spread the cost of injuries among a large group of consumers as a part of an ongoing business. In addition, the person running the yard sale will have no ability to work to improve the design of the products being sold. As such, a person having a yard sale is not considered in the business of selling the products and will not, therefore, be subject to strict liability.

Understanding that the defendant is a "business seller" of the product is a necessary first step to understanding the basic elements of strict liability. The details of exactly who is considered a "business seller" is, of course, complicated. The examples given above are simply by way of illustration. More detail about the appropriate parties to products liability litigation is contained in Chapter 6 below.

3. Product

It probably sounds overly simplistic to state but strict liability for products liability injuries is limited to injuries caused by products. Other areas of the law may use other similar terms to describe what can be covered by strict liability. In property law, the courts may speak of chattels while in cases concerning the Uniform Commercial Code the courts may speak of the "sale of goods." Strict liability for product injuries requires that the injury causing item be "product," "chattel," or "goods." Clearly strict liability for products liability cases should not be concerned with injury caused on real estate. In addition, when professionals provide service to clients, that is not sale of a product. When a physician diagnosis a disease, that may be malpractice for which negligence is appropriate, but strict liability does not apply.

Some simple examples may be observed. When a retailer sells a toaster to a customer, that is the sale of a product. Strict liability would be an available remedy for an injury. The reason that the Uniform Commercial Code warranties may also be used in this setting is that it is also the sale of "goods." If, however, a seller of 100 acres of farm land was sued because the purchaser fell in a hole on the land, that would not be appropriate for strict liability. That was a sale of real property and not a product.

The definition of the word product, however, can be more difficult. When a manufacturer sells items that become fixed to a home, thereby becoming "fixtures," those products start to meet the definition of real estate. When the manufacturer of a mobile home sells, delivers and hooks up the home to the utilities, that home begins to look more like real estate. In those examples, however, some courts may still find the item sold to be a product. In addition, when a contractor builds a whole subdivision of identical homes, the homes look like real property. A court, however, may find that the homes were mass produced more in the nature of products. Finally, some professionals use or transfer products to clients during the course of professional treatment. A physician may, for example, place a heart pacemaker in the chest of a patient with heart rhythm problems. If the pacemaker proves to be defective, the question arises as to whether the transfer of the pacemaker was the sale of a product or merely a transfer incidental to professional service. That example would probably treat the transfer as part of the service and limit the physician's liability to one based on negligence. Other service/sale examples, however, have created greater difficulty. More of those examples will be discussed in detail in Chapter 6, below.

As can be seen, the simple statement of the element is that in order for strict liability to apply, the injury must have arisen from a product. Defining what is meant by a "product" can, at times, be difficult.

4. Defective Condition

In order to use strict liability for product injuries, the product must be "defective." Substantial debate occurred during the drafting of Restatement (Second) of Torts § 402A on how to define when a strict liability action could be brought. The basic understanding was that sellers would not be insurers of the safety of the product. Such defendants would not be liable every time a product caused an injury. Such sellers would only be liable when there was something wrong with the product. A good example would be the use of a simple kitchen butcher knife. If a user cut his or her finger with the knife due to being careless with the use, that should not lead to liability. If, however, the knife blade broke off during normal use due to impurities in the metal, and the broken portion of the blade hit the user causing injury, that should lead to liability. In an effort to distinguish such cases, the American Law Institute came up with the language that the product had to be in a "defective condition unreasonably dangerous."

Although many jurisdictions use that phrase, "defective condition unreasonably dangerous," as a single statement of the test, it may be easier to understand by breaking in down into two parts. For an initial study, understanding this most critical portion of strict liability may be easier by seeing the problem as one requiring (1) defective condition, and (2) unreasonably dangerous. Final analysis will, of course, require putting those concepts together.

In terms of "defective condition," a product may be defective in one of three ways. A product may be defective due to (1) a failure in the manufacturing process, (2) an improper design, or (3) a failure to fully warn about the risks of the product.

The mis-manufacturing defect may be the easiest to understand. A mis-manufactured product is one that is not as originally designed or intended by the seller. Even though that description sounds like it is moving towards something like intent, it is not. This type of defect has been the one most consistently found by jurisdictions capable of being tested by strict liability. There is no requirement of proving that the manufacturer knew or failed to use reasonable care to know that the product did not meet the original design standards.

These types of cases may be frequently seen as failures of quality assurance. Most manufacturers try to make products as designed. Most manufacturers may have teams of quality assurance personnel that run checks to make sure products are made correctly. It appears, however, that no amount of checking will produce a perfect product every time. Products slip through the manufacturing process with something done incorrectly. When this occurs, the manufacturer is liable in strict liability.

It is not only the manufacturer that may be strictly liable. Any seller in the chain of distribution may also be strictly liable. They too have sold a product that is defective.

This defect is frequently the easiest to prove. Although there is further discussion about this topic in Chapter 7 below, examples may be seen. When a product malfunctions, it gives rise to an inference that there is something wrong with it. Toasters, for example, toast bread, they do not catch on fires. When one catches on fire, it appears defective.

Defective design cases are usually much more difficult cases for both plaintiffs and defendants. In such cases, the plaintiff admits that the product was manufactured exactly at intended by the designers of the product. The allegation by the plaintiff is that the design itself was defective. Ordinarily, this requires that the plaintiff prove that the product could have been designed in a better, safer manner.

These cases require expert testimony. The plaintiffs will use experts to prove that the design was defective and the cause of the injuries. The defendants will offer experts to prove that the design was not defective.

The critical feature of most of these cases is the question of feasible alternative. The plaintiff will ordinarily be required to prove that a different design could have been used. The concept of feasible alternative usually means that it was technically and economically feasible to create a safer design. The defendants will usually offer evidence that the design could not have been safer. In fact, defendants will usually offer evidence that the product was designed at the "state of the art" at the time the product was manufactured.

As the most difficult cases for plaintiffs to prove, plaintiffs routinely add other allegations to design defect claims. A typical action includes both a design defect claim and a failure to warn claim. Before proceeding to an overview of warning claims, please note that a further discussion of design defect claims appears in Chapter 8, below.

Failure to warn claims provide the third type of defect. Such claims allege that the product is defective because the manufacturer failed to provide adequate instructions or warnings concerning the risks associated with the product. Although the failure to warn allegations may be added to manufacturing defect claims or design defect claims, they may also be used to stand alone. The plaintiff may be willing to admit that the design is adequate and the product was manufactured properly. The sole claim can be that the user was injured due to a lack of information about how to use the product safely.

After the adoption of Restatement (Second) of Torts § 402A, it appeared that failure to warn cases could be tried in strict liability. That would, of course, have required that the defendant be liable for failure to have an adequate warning with no proof of fault. Courts have not found that position to be satisfactory. Courts have routinely indicated that defendants have a duty to warn, but only of foreseeable risks of harm. By adding the element of having to prove the foreseeable risk of harm, the action appears to be one of negligence.

Failure to warn cases have covered all types of products. The least complex household tool comes complete with multiple warnings. Of course, more complex products have lengthy warnings. (A further discussion of failure to warn cases appears in Chapter 9, below.)

5. Unreasonably Dangerous

As noted above, the American Law Institute debated for some time about how to further define the nature of the defect that would lead to liability. The term chosen was "defective condition unreasonably dangerous." The problem with the term, however, is that the use of the word "unreasonable" makes it appear to be a question of negligence. The case is not to be one of negligence.

To distinguish between negligence and strict liability a simple explanation is needed. Negligence focuses on the nature of the conduct of the parties. In a negligence product liability action, the concern would be whether the seller had failed to use reasonable care. In strict liability, the concern is the nature of the product. There is no issue of whether the seller used reasonable care. The only question is whether the product is reasonably safe.

After adopting § 402, courts worked to develop a test to explain how to measure the dangerousness of a product. Those tests are further discussed In subsection B, below of this chapter.

6. Without Substantial Change

Restatement (Second) of Torts § 402A notes that the product must reach the user or consumer "without substantial change." This is a way of saying that the product must have had the defect when it left the hands of the defendant. If the defect was added to the product after it left the hands of the defendant, then the defendant is not liable for the harm.

There are, of course, numerous ways that a defect can enter a product after it has left the hands of the defendant. It could have been altered by the plaintiff or some third party. It could have simply aged and become defective with the naturally process of "wearing out." Any of those would be sufficient to defeat an action in strict liability.

7. Users or Consumers

Strict liability for products case uses the simple concept of "users or consumers" to define the proper party plaintiff. Although negligence actions once required privity, the proper plaintiff in most tort cases is now the "foreseeable plaintiff." The phrase "user or consumer" is usually seen as the same as the "foreseeable plaintiff."

Examples of the user or consumer are easy to understand. Obviously, the purchaser of a product is a user or consumer. In addition, family, friends or others who may use the product would meet the definition. Bystanders have also been included within the phrase user or consumer. Passengers in automobiles or even pedestrian injured by defective automobiles can be included.

8. Physical Harm

The final basic element requires that the recover for harm must be for some physical harm to the user or property of the user. Those elements require some explanation.

Physical harm to the user includes the traditional personal injury losses. Medical bills, lost wages, and pain and suffering are examples of those traditional losses. Any of those that were caused by the defect in the product may be recovered.

It is also recognized that a product may cause harm to other property. When a household appliance catches on fire, it may also damage the house. When an automobile is defective, it may hit another automobile and cause damage to that auto. Each of those would be examples of damage to other property and would be recoverable for strict liability in tort.

Strict liability does not allow recovery for pure economic losses. For recovery of those, the plaintiff would need to bring a warranty claim. An easy example of such a claim would be where a purchaser has a defective truck. Due to the defect in the truck, the business in which the truck was being used was unable to operate while the truck was being repaired. The lost business and profits for the time lost would be considered a pure economic loss. That loss would not be liable in strict liability.

The harder claim is when the defective product causes damage to itself. It appears, to some, that such damage is an injury to property. Since a product is property, it would appear that damage should be recoverable in strict liability. After some early splits of authority, courts now agree that such claims are not recoverable in strict liability. Where the claim is for the reduced value of the product itself, that claim is not recoverable in strict liability. The plaintiff would need a warranty claim.

B. Tests for Unreasonably Dangerous

The most difficult issue in the claim for strict liability is determining when a product is in a defective condition unreasonably dangerous. The Restatement itself suggested one possible test while courts have developed others. Although these tests have been developed primarily in the design defect cases, some courts across the country have used them in all types of defect cases. It is important to be able to understand and apply all of the available tests. Different jurisdictions use different tests and some jurisdictions use combinations of several. It is also not uncommon for jurisdictions to change the test that is to be applied.

1. Consumer Expectation

The first test, and, for some time the only test, was the consumer expectation test. This test was, in fact, suggested by the comments to Restatement (Second) of Torts § 402A. The test to be answered by this theory is whether the product performed in a manner as expected by the ordinarily prudent consumer.

The consumer expectation test had several distinct advantages. It allowed the jury to approach the issue as one from the reasonable person's understanding. Jurors could understand what an ordinary consumer would expect of most products. Consumers would expect, for example, a toaster to toast bread but would not expect that toaster to burn down the house. Jurors could even apply a simple risk utility analysis to such a test. Most consumers would expect that very expensive product would perform better and last longer then a cheaply made copy of the same type of product. This test also made it simple for the jurors to focus on the condition of the product rather than the conduct of the manufacturer. Since the claim is suppose to be based on strict liability, the condition of the product is supposed to be the critical issue.

It rapidly became obvious, however, that the consumer expectation test was flawed. It did not work well for more complex cases. Courts became concerned that consumers just did not have expectations about complex products. Although jurors could have ordinary expectations about toasters, jurors would be confused by the details of products such as automobiles. Fully understanding the performance characteristics of such products could only be understood by experts.

Due to this concern about the problem with the consumer expectation test, courts and text writers began to formulate different tests. Recognizing that risk/utility has always been a part of tort law and could even figure into a consumer expectation test, such an analysis took shape for strict liability in products cases.

2. Risk-Utility

A simple risk/utility analysis began to take shape as concerns about the consumer expectation test arose. Text writers and courts began to suggest that jurors should just be asked to compare the utility of the product against the risks that such a product created. Courts have been adopting such an approach.

The risk/utility is easy to explain and use in trial. The jury is just instructed that they are to measure the risks created by the product defect and compare those risks to the utility of the product. If the risks exceed the utility, then the product is unreasonably dangerous. If the utility exceeds the risks, then the product is not unreasonably dangerous.

This test, as did the consumer expectation test, allows the jury to focus on the condition of the product and not be concerned with the reasonableness of the care of the manufacturer. This assures that the test remains one of strict liability and not negligence.

Obviously this test would require extensive expert testimony. Jurors would not be able to measure the relative risks and utilities of complex products without experts giving evidence. This would be especially true of design defect cases. Where a plaintiff claimed that a better design would reduce risks and increase utility, experts in the field would be necessary to explain the reasoning.

It may seem that a product with any risk associate with its use should be declared an unreasonably dangerous product. That, however, would make the manufacturer and insurer of the safety of the user and not leave the issue as merely one of strict liability. There are many products generally available on the market today that have a high degree of risk associated with use, but are still of great utility. Most hand tools, for example, may be extremely dangerous. Saws must be sharp in order to cut wood. Although that sharpness does create some risks, the need for saws in the modern world is high. Even the simple kitchen butcher knife has a high degree of risk associated with its use. Modern cooks, however, could not prepare meals without this knife. Although it has a risk, the utility is much higher. Those are just some simple examples of common products that have a utility that exceeds the risks associated with their use. Such products would not be unreasonably dangerous just because of the inherent risks in their use.

The desire to move to a risk utility analysis left some text writers concerned about the proper manner to instruct the jury. Some felt that merely instructing on risks and utilities would not be appropriate.

3. Knowledgeable Manufacturer

As jurisdictions began to move to a risk utility analysis, text writers explored methods to use to instruct the jury on such a theory. Dean Wade of Vanderbilt University developed a method that was adopted by some jurisdictions as a way of using the risk utility analysis without specifically mentioning risks and utilities.

The problem was to continue to focus on the condition of the product and not allow the court or jury to consider the reasonableness of the conduct of the manufacturer. At the same time, it was thought to be advantageous to use language that had been developed during the growth of negligence law. Combining those concerns allowed the creation of what could be called a "knowledgeable manufacturer" test.

The knowledgeable manufacturer test created a jury instruction. At the close of the trial the jury would be instructed to ASSUME the manufacturer had knowledge of the risks associated with the product and then decide whether a reasonable manufacturer would have put the product on the market.

At first glance, it appears that this test merely adopts negligence. It clearly asks what a reasonable manufacturer would have done. It must be noted, however, that the instruction requires the jury to ASSUME the manufacturer had knowledge of the risk. This places a degree of knowledge on the defendant that the defendant did not have. The defendant may not have known the product was dangerous. (Obviously, if the seller had known of dangerous risks and continue to market the product, the conduct may well have been negligent. In strict liability, however, it does not matter whether the seller knew or not. That knowledge will be assumed.) Even without the actual knowledge, the seller will be placed in the position of the jury assuming that knowledge was there and then asking whether a reasonable manufacturer would place the product on the market.

The use of "assumed knowledge" again lets the jury focus on the condition of the product. The actual conduct of the manufacturer is not relevant. The key to the case is what ordinarily prudent sellers would have done once they did have that knowledge.

It may appear that this would always require a plaintiff's verdict. If the seller is assumed to have known of risks, would not the seller refuse to sell the product? Again not all dangerous products are unreasonably dangerous. As suggested in the section on risk utility analysis, some products are dangerous but are needed in society. Even assuming that sellers know saws and butcher knives are sharp, ordinarily prudent sellers will continue to sell them. They are needed in society.

It is clear that the knowledgeable manufacturer test is merely another way of explaining risk utility. By using the knowledgeable ordinarily prudent manufacturer as the key, jurors are invited to weigh the risks and utilities of a product. Again, extensive amounts of expert testimony will be necessary in such cases.

4. Combinations

The above three tests appear to be the methods that courts are using to determine whether a product is in a defective condition unreasonably dangerous. Jurisdictions have tended to pick one of the tests and use it. The consumer expectation test was the first and only test immediately after the adoption of Restatement (Second) of Torts § 402A. The use of some form of risk/utility analysis is now probably the majority rule.

Some jurisdictions have chosen to use a combination of the above tests. California, for example, uses a combination of the consumer expectation test and the risk utility analysis. That jurisdiction provides a good example of such combined uses.

In California, the jury is ultimately instructed on both the consumer expectation test and the risk/utility analysis. The key to the case is the burden of proof. In the initial stages, the plaintiff has the burden of proving that the product fails to meet the ordinary consumer expectations. If the plaintiff meets that burden, the burden shifts to the defendant to prove that the utility of the product exceeds the risk. This method of deciding strict liability does not actually create a new test, but it does allow the jurisdiction to combine some of the best features of different tests. A small number of states have followed California in using this combination.

C. Proof Problems

The preceding material in this chapter has discussed the basic elements of strict liability for product cases. The difficulty with those elements, of course, is that the facts must be proven to meet those elements. With few exceptions, the burden of proof on every element of the claim is on the plaintiff. A few specific proof problems that the plaintiff must face should be discussed.

1. Defect in the Product

Proving that there is a defect in a product is one of the difficult issues for strict liability. It will, in most instances, require the use of expert testimony. The nature of that testimony will be dependent on the type of defect that the plaintiff is trying to prove. For design defects, the expert will have to show how the product could have been designed with feasible alternatives. For manufacturing defects, the experts will have to show how the product in question differed from the whole product line. For warning defects, it will be necessary to show how a better warning would have allowed the plaintiff to use the product more safely.

There are cases, however, where certain inferences may assist the parties to the litigation. Those inferences ordinarily help the plaintiff.

In failure to warn cases, there is always an issue of causation. The plaintiff must show that the presence of a better warning would have allowed safer use of the product. This may require that the plaintiff first show that the warning would have been read. Courts will tend to use a "read and heed" presumptions. Such a theory will presume that the plaintiff would have read any warnings that would have been present.

A more interesting inference is one that seems similar to res ipsa loquitur. It must be remembered, of course, that res ipsa loquitur is an inference that allows the proof of breach in a negligence case. It does not prove anything in a strict liability case. There are cases, however, where the failure of a product to operate gives rise to an inference of a defect. When, for example, a toaster catches on fire, there is an inference that the toaster would not have done that if it had not been defective. Courts do not like to infer the existence of a defect and proof may be necessary. It is only in rare, simple cases that such an inference will operate.

Frequently plaintiffs are confronted with the further problem of proving exactly which defect caused the injury. A product may leave the experts confused as to what exactly occurred. Some experts may be convinced that the product had multiple defects but are unable to point to the specific defect that caused the injury. Such cases are frequently found in favor of the defendant. Plaintiffs can win such cases, however, with additional proof. After showing the multiple defects that were possible, the experts must be able to discount the possibility of non-defect issues causing the injury. By showing a range of defects and pointing out that the injury must have been caused by at least one of the defects, many courts will let the case go to the jury.

Showing the possibility of multiple defects also raises the problem of even showing that a defect was in the product before the accident. Two simple problems frequently complicate the plaintiff's cases. In order for the expert to be able to study the product and reach an opinion, the product must be available. Frequently, after an accident with a product, the product is disposed of. The injured plaintiff will not be thinking of litigation while going through the initial trauma of seeking medical help. It may months later that the injured party realizes that the product should have been saved. In addition, once a product fails and causes injury, the product may be further destroyed by the accident. Imagine, for example, and automobile accident that shows that an axle is broken after the accident. The plaintiff's expert may claim that the axle broke and caused the accident. The defendant's expert may claim that the plaintiff carelessly drove the automobile into a ditch and the accident caused the axle to be broken. As those examples illustrate, just preserving the evidence may be difficult.

2. Unreasonably Dangerous

The discussion of "unreasonably dangerous" that appears in the prior portions of this chapter should illustrate that this issue is the most difficult issue in strict liability. The nature of the proof will depend on the nature of the claimed defect. Regardless of the nature of the proof, it will require experts.

If the alleged defect is a design defect, then the plaintiffs will be faced with using experts to meet the test that is selected by the jurisdiction. The expert will have to frame the evidence in terms either of "consumer expectation," "knowledgeable manufacturer," or "risk utility."

Although some jurisdictions use those above tests for all forms of defects, proof of a manufacturing defect may be somewhat easier. Proof that the product is not like others in the product line is frequently sufficient to get the case to the jury. Such proof is usually easier.

Warning defects have both advantages and disadvantages. Usually courts find it easy to say that a better warning would have been preferred. It does not take much of an expert to draft a better warning. Frequently, however, plaintiffs may find it useful to use different types of industrial engineers to point out current trends in safety warnings.

3. Need for Expert Testimony

As noted above, most products liability cases require the use of expert testimony. The law concerning the use of experts has gotten increasing complex and will be discussed in Chapter 11. For the parties to the litigation, one of the major issues may be cost. For a plaintiff, the case is probably being litigated on a contingency fee. The plaintiff's attorney will have to provide the up-front cost to the litigation in hopes of recovering fees and costs if the action is successful. In addition, many experts already work for manufacturers and product designers. They will not be available for plaintiffs. Plaintiffs will be seeking expensive experts that are not currently being used in the industry that is being sued

Defendants have greater advantages in seeking experts. At least for the manufacturers, they already start with the expert team that designed the product that was sold. Although using the design team for litigation is an expensive use of time and takes the experts away from the primary focus of their jobs in designing new products, at least the defendants have access to experts.

Strict Liability Checkpoints

- The basic elements of Restatement (Second) of Torts § 402A are:
  - A business seller; of
  - A product; in
  - A defective condition;
  - Unreasonably dangerous;
  - To a user or consumer; and
  - Reaches that user or consumer without substantial change; and
  - Causes physical harm to that user or consumer's person or other property.
- The tests that are applied for "unreasonably dangerous" are:
  - The "Consumer Expectation" Test; and
  - A risk-utility analysis; and
  - A "Knowledgeable Manufacturer" Test; and
  - Combinations of those tests.

Chapter 4

Warranty

Warranty Roadmap

- Learn the basic types of warranties.
- Understand the elements of each type of warranty.

A. Introduction

Warranty claims are actions that seem more related to contract than tort. It may even seem odd to be studying a contract/Uniform Commercial Code topic in what arises in consumer product safety cases. Products liability actions, however, contain both tort and contract features. They appear to be tort claims because they typically arise when a plaintiff has suffered a personal injury or property damage. The contract nature of the claim arises, however, since the product was typically sold in the course of business and did not perform as expected. Plaintiffs' attorneys will typically bring the action based on tort and contract theories. The previous chapter noted the most common tort theories. Those theories are, of course, negligence and strict liability. This chapter covers the most common contract theories. Those theories are included under the broad heading of warranty.

In the products liability action there is the possibility of three different types of warranty claims. One of those claims is the express warranty. The other two claims are implied warranties. Under the implied warranties, the claim may be based on the implied warranty of merchantability or the implied warranty of fitness for a particular purpose. Each of those claims have specific elements that must be met. The following chapter discusses those elements. (For a lesson on warranties, see CALI Lessons, Warranties, http://www2.cali.org)

B. Express

Express warranties are, in some ways, the simplest form of warranty to understand. They appear to be similar to the tort claim in misrepresentation. The basic requirements of an express warranty claim is that the plaintiff prove that there was a false statement of fact which was a part of the sale which led to the injury.

The Uniform Commercial Code indicates that there are three ways that a seller can make an express warranty. Obviously when the seller makes an affirmation of fact or a promise about the way the product will perform, that is an express warranty. In addition, the express warranty may be created by a sale by sample or a description of the product. These methods provide a broad range of express warranties. It is important to note that no special words are necessary to create an express warranty. It is not required that the seller use the phrase "warranty" or "guarantee." The warranty can be created without those particular words.

The affirmation of fact or promise is a basic way that an express warranty may be created. When the seller states something about the product, that is an express warranty. It is not necessary that the affirmation be in writing. It may be oral. The affirmation of fact or promise express warranty does, however, create some issues. The most obvious is the distinction between facts and opinions. It is well know that sellers of product, at times, engage in "sales puffing." They may exaggerate the qualities of the product to the extent that no one would actually believe the remarks. Such opinions are not actionable. Difficult issues can arise with the jury being asked to decide if the statement was a fact or an opinion. One typical affirmation that has arisen in numerous cases is the statement that the product is "new." Sellers have been known to take a slightly used product and sell it as new. Such a statement is an affirmation of fact and can be actionable.

A second method of creating an express warranty is to sell the product with a description. This method will, at times, seem to overlap with the affirmation of fact or promise. When a seller describes a product, that may also appear to be an affirmation of fact. By claiming a product is "new," the seller is describing and affirming something about that product. Other examples of sales by description may also be seen. Making statements about the size or capacity of the product would be a description. There is no reason to be overly concerned about the differences between affirmations and sales by descriptions. Either and both will result in express warranties.

The third method of creating an express warranty is a sale by sample. It is not uncommon for a seller to provide samples or examples of a product that the purchasers want to order. Such sales create an express warranty that the product will be consistent with the sample or model.

It should be noted again that the language of the Uniform Commercial Code is broad enough to include many types of sales circumstances. When a seller provides brochures, books, photographs, diagrams, pictures, descriptions, video tapes, or any other method of encouraging the sale of the product, that may well be found to be an express warranty by the courts.

Once it is found that an express warranty has been created, there is one additional element that must be met in order for it to be actionable. The express warranty must be a part of the "basis of the bargain." This phrase has let to confusion in the law. Under the older Uniform Sales Act and most tort misrepresentation claims, the law requires that false statements be relied upon. Reliance is a critical element of those claims. The drafter of the Uniform Commercial Code, however, chose not to use the term "reliance," and, instead, used the phrase "basis of the bargain." This change created the confusion.

Courts have used several methods to explain the phrase "basis of the bargain." One extreme felt that the deletion of the term reliance showed an intention to broaden the law substantially. That theory holds that there is no element of reliance in express warranty claims. For those jurisdictions, when the seller creates an express warranty, it becomes a part of the basis of the bargain and is actionable without further proof by the buyer. The other extreme view takes the position that the drafters of the Uniform Commercial Code did not intend such an extreme view. For those jurisdictions, the courts still require the element of reliance. They do, however, require the seller to prove the absence of reliance in order to avoid liability rather than requiring buyers to prove reliance in order to recover.

A few specific examples have created difficulties for the "basis of the bargain" issue. Where, for example, the affirmation appears in an advertisement which the buyer did not see, it is hard to imagine that the statement was a part of the basis of the bargain. Courts would be more likely to require reliance in such a case. Likewise, where the statement was made after the sale, it seems that the affirmation is not a "basis of the bargain." It would seem likely that the buyer would have to prove something like reliance.

C. Implied

Implied warranties may also give rise to a claim by the plaintiff. Such warranties do not require specific words or actions, but are, instead, created by the sale itself. In some ways, it may be said that such implied warranties "run with the product." The law will create two types of implied warranties. Those two types of implied warranties are fitness for particular purpose and merchantability.

1. Fitness

The implied warranty of fitness for a particular purpose is a narrow, limited warranty. As suggested by the name, it is intended to apply to a "particular purpose" for which the user obtained it. This warranty has several elements that must be closed viewed.

The implied warranty of fitness for a particular purpose has two major elements. In order to recover, the user must prove that (1) the seller knew or had reason to know of the particular purposes for which the product was being selected, and (2) the user relied upon the expertise of the seller in selecting the product.

The first element requires that the seller know or have reason to know of the particular purposes for which the user is obtaining the product. In many typical consumer sales that element will not be met. When a buyer goes to a department store to buy a toaster, the buyer rarely tells the seller of some particular purpose. In many department stores, the buyer cannot find a sales associate to talk to. The buyer will look on the shelves and select a toaster. The sales associate that rings up the sale never knows or has reason to know of any particular purpose. (Notice also that the buyer does not rely on the seller in the selection in such sales.)

It is not enough for the seller to know of general purposes. The warranty requires the knowledge of specific purposes. If, for example, the buyer asked a sales associate where the toasters were located and the sales associate said, "They are in aisle number 8," that would not create this warranty. The seller may know or have reason to know of the general need for a toaster, but would not know of any particularized need.

A good example of a particular purpose could involve a toaster. A buyer might find a sales associate and say, "I own a small diner and need a toaster to handle the breakfast crowd. I usually get about 25 people for breakfast. I need to toast about 2 slices of bread for each. I also have to toast up about 5 bagels each morning." At that point, the sales associate would know of have reason to know of specific needs of the buyer. The buyer is looking for a restaurant quality toaster and not a home use toaster. The next question would be whether the buyer then relies upon the seller in selecting the toaster?

The next element requires that the buyer rely upon the seller for selecting the product. The question of reliance is usually one of fact and can be difficult to prove. Frequently the buyer will ask for the seller's advice, then inspect the product before purchasing it. It is not necessary that the buyer give total reliance on the sellers advice, but there should be substantial reliance. Where the buyer asks for advice, but makes the purchase decision based upon his or her own inspection, there would be no implied warranty of fitness.

In the above example of the diner owner seeking to purchase the toaster, an example of reliance may be seen. If, after the diner owner made the statements about the need for a toaster, the buyer handed over one particular toaster and the buyer purchased it, then there would be an implied warranty of fitness for particular purpose.

It is, of course, rare for a sales associate to hand over a product and say nothing. Frequently, the sales associate would do something like hand over the toaster and then say, "This one will do the job for you." Notice that such an additional statement would add an express warranty claim. It is often that a purchaser will have both an express warranty and the implied warranty of fitness claim in the same action.

In short, the implied warranty of fitness for a particular purpose is narrow because of the two elements discussed. The plaintiff must prove both that the seller knew or had reason to know of the particular use and that the plaintiff relied upon the seller in selecting the product. In the typical consumer goods transaction, that does not occur.

2. Merchantability

An implied warranty that ordinarily attaches to all sales in a products liability setting is the implied warranty of merchantability. This implied warranty is much broader and can frequently be used in the typical product liability setting. In use, the implied warranty of merchantability is similar to strict liability in tort under Restatement (Second) of Torts § 402A.

A good way to understand the basic idea behind the implied warranty of merchantability is to compare it to the implied warranty of fitness for a particular purpose. The implied warranty of fitness for a particular purpose assumes that the buyer has some special or particular purpose for which the product will be used. The implied warranty of fitness then "warrants" that the product will serve that purpose. The implied warranty of merchantability assumes that the warranty is to extend to general purposes or uses of the product. This implied warranty "warrants" that the product will serve those general purposes. Notice, for example, the toaster discussed in the implied warranty of fitness section. In that section, the buyer wanted a toaster that could be used in a commercial, restaurant setting. The implied warranty of fitness could be used for that setting. The implied warranty of merchantability would cover the general uses of toasting bread, but would not "warrant" that the toaster would hold up to the extreme uses in a restaurant.

The Uniform Commercial Code does not give a good definition of merchantability, but, instead, gives a list of examples of what merchantability includes. That list is in U.C.C. § 2-314. Some of the items appear to be more associated with major commercial transactions and do not arise often in consumer product sales. There are a few, however, that seem to speak directly to such sales. The terms of merchantability include:

U.C.C. 2-314:

(c) are fit for ordinarily purposes for which such goods are used; and

(d) run, within the variations permitted by the agreement, of even kind, quality and quantity within each unit and among all units involved; and

(e) are adequately contained, packaged, and labeled as the agreement may require; and

(f) conform to the promises or affirmations of fact make on the container or label if any.

The item (c) above seems to capture the underlying idea for the implied warranty of merchantability as applied to products liability cases. When a consumer is using a product, there is a warranty that the product will be "fit for ordinary purposes."

This implied warranty "runs" with the product. The warranty attaches unless it is specifically disclaimed or limited. There is no requirement of agreement for the warranty to attach and no requirement of reliance. In these ways, this warranty is broader then both express warranty and the implied warranty of fitness.

There is an important limitation on the implied warranty of merchantability. The warranty only attaches when the sale is from a "merchant with respect to goods of that kind." U.C.C. 2-314. This warranty requires a "merchant," and that "merchant" must be a merchant of the goods the type of which are the subject to the litigation. It is easy to see the obvious examples. If a customer wanted to buy a toaster and went into a discount store that stocked and sold toasters, that discount store would be a merchant of goods of that kind. If, however, the customer sought to buy a toaster at a yard sale being held by a neighbor, that neighbor is not a "merchant" of toasters. Purchasing an automobile is another easy example. If a customer goes to the new car dealership to purchase a new car, that dealership is a merchant of goods of that kind. If, however, the customer buys a used car from a neighbor, that neighbor is not a merchant of goods of that kind. It should be noted that the term "merchant" is similar to the use of the term "business seller" in strict liability actions under the Restatement (Second) of Torts § 402A. Both require that the seller be in the business of selling such goods.

Harder cases have appeared in trying to determine whether a seller is a merchant of goods of that kind. Banks, for example, are in the business of banking. That includes the business of making automobile loans. If a bank had to repossess an automobile for non-payment of the loan and then resell that automobile, the question could arise as to whether the bank was a merchant of automobiles. It would appear that the bank is not. If, however, a seller was in the business of buying and selling used automobiles, even if some of those were obtained from bank repossessions, that seller would be in the business of selling used automobiles. Such a seller of used automobiles is a merchant of goods of that kind.

D. Special Contract Problems

The above material covers the basic elements of the warranties that are important to products liability actions. Since warranties are in the nature of contract claims, there are some special problems that distinguish them from tort claims. A few of these problems should be noted here and in subsequent chapters on Parties (Chapter 6), Defenses (Chapter 12), and Damages (Chapter 13).

1. Notice

A traditional requirement of contract law is that the plaintiff should give notice to a prospective defendant in the case of a breach of contract. The purpose of such notice should be obvious. Such notice gives the prospective defendant the chance to try to correct the breach and limit or mitigate some of the damages. This might be especially important in a product liability setting. If the product has a dangerous design or warning defect, it would be good for the public safety for the manufacturer to have notice promptly in order to start making corrections or issuing recalls.

The problems with the notice requirement in a products liability setting should be equally obvious. Although commercial buyer and sellers may know of the need to give notice, the typical consumer may not. If a consumer is injured by a product, that consumer may not even consider litigation for some time. In addition, the consumer may not realize that it is important to give notice to prospective parties. The consumer may think to return to a store to complain about the product, but may fail to give notice to other parties in the chain of distribution. Finally, the injured party may be a bystander and not the original purchaser. That bystander may not think of the necessity of giving notice.

This apparent conflict between the needs of the defendant to have prompt notice and the reality of the fact that the plaintiff may not have been aware of that requirement has led to some conflict between cases. There is not a good way to identify the specific time period in which the consumer must give notice.

The Uniform Commercial Code § 2-607 indicates that the party seeking to claim a breach of warranty must give notice within a "reasonable" time. By use of the term "reasonable," the code allows the courts to strike a balance between the conflicting needs of the parties. This has been especially true of consumer and bystander plaintiffs. The courts have tended to recognize that such parties may have clearly been unaware of the need to give notice. It is, of course, important for attorneys representing such clients to give notice as promptly as possible after coming into contact with the case. Some courts have been lenient and allowed actions to proceed even when notice was delayed for a few years.

2. Economic Losses

The possibility of recovering pure economic losses is one of the reasons that plaintiffs' lawyers may chose to use a warranty claim. In suing in tort, the plaintiff is limited to recover for personal injury or property damages. There is no recover for pure economic losses. There are times, for example, that the destruction of a product may also mean that a consumer could loose profits in a business. The owner of a truck may find that business has to be limited while a defective truck is being repaired. In addition, the courts have recognized that the loss of value of the product itself is an economic loss. So recover of damages for repair of the product is not recoverable in tort in most jurisdictions. Recognizing those shortcomings, plaintiffs' attorneys can use the warranty claims.

Using the warranty claims, plaintiffs can recover for the loss profits and the losses to the value of the product itself. It should be noted, that the Uniform Commercial Code does not limit recover to economic losses. The plaintiff can also recover "consequential losses" in the nature of other property damage and personal injury for breach of warranty. By allowing such a broad range of recovery, most plaintiffs' lawyers find it advantageous to add warranty claims to all products liability actions. Their hope is that all damages will then be recoverable and there will be multiple bases of recover for some of the losses suffered.

3. Disclaimers

The idea behind disclaimers is consistent with the general theory of contract law. Parties to a contract should be able to agree to the terms and conditions of that contract. Those parties should be able to accept or reject any terms as long as they both agree. With that theory in place, the parties to a contract should be able to agree to accept warranties or agree to void all warranties.

Although that underlying theory seems obvious for contract law there is a problem in some types of cases. Where the parties to a contract are both commercial entities and each has its own team of engineers and lawyers, agreeing to dispense with all warranties makes sense. The buyer can have his or her own engineers study the product and get a full explanation of the law from lawyers. Where the transaction is between a consumer and a large manufacturer or retailers, however, the ability to disclaim warranties is more troublesome.

The typical consumer is not able to fully understand the engineering, design, and manufacturing of a product that may be purchased. That consumer will not be able to figure out the full quality of the product. In addition, if the language of the sales agreement contains technical, legal terms, the ordinary consumer will not fully understand what the legal impact of those terms are.

With the difference that can exist between the commercial transaction and the consumer purchase, the Uniform Commercial Code has sought to strike a balance. The parties to a contract of sale may disclaim warranties but there are protections for the ordinary consumer.

Express warranties exist when a seller makes an affirmation or promise, a sale by description or a sale by sample. There may be times when such a seller then seeks to disclaim the express warranty. It would seem that an attempt to disclaim would be the most troubling example. Imagine a contract of sale for a product which had a list of express promises on the front of the document and then a disclaimer of all promises on the back of the document. The Uniform Commercial Code indicates that when there is an express warranty and words that appear to limit or disclaim the express warranty, the language of those items shall be read, when possible, to be consistent. Where such language is not consistent, language tending to limit or disclaim the warranty shall be inoperative. (Uniform Commercial Code § 2-316(1).)

The relationship between express warranties and disclaimers, therefore, is clear. Where there is an inconsistency in the language, the express warranty still stands. It appears that the Uniform Commercial Code makes it impossible to disclaim express warranties. Although this is very close to being accurate, the problem must be considered closely.

The language of the U.C.C. does not specifically say that express warranties cannot be disclaimed. It does say that the limitation language and the warranty language will be interpreted consistently where reasonably possible. The reason for this is to allow the seller to expressly warranty some items but not others. The seller may clearly make an express warranty for part of the product, for some products, or for some period of time, while refusing to warrant everything for all time. A good example of such a warranty can be found in the sale of most new automobiles. A new automobile may warrant the paint for 1 year or 12,000 miles, while providing a warranty on the drive train of the automobile for 3 years or 36,000 miles. Such a warranty would be seen as an express warranty and would call in the need to consider the language for its consistency. There does not appear to be anything inconsistent with the language. If a buyer wanted warranty coverage for the paint for 3 years, the court could easily decline. There is nothing unreasonably inconsistent about providing different warranties for different things. If, however, after listing those warranties on the front of the sales contract, the back of the contract said, "This contract contains no express warranties," that final provision would not be enforced. That would be held to be inconsistent with the warranties given on the front of the contract.

Implied warranties have their own special difficulties when they are a part of consumer sales. Commercial buyers will have teams of lawyers to tell them that there are implied warranties that go with the sale. Consumer purchasers probably do not realize there is even such a thing as an implied warranty. It is the disclaimer of implied warranties, therefore, that give rise to the greatest danger of confusion by the consumer.

The U.C.C. does allow the seller to completely disclaim both of the implied warranties. (U.C.C. 2-316). In order to protect the consumer, the U.C.C. has a series of requirements that are intended to put the consumer on notice that something important is happening. It is hoped that the consumer will read language about implied warranties being disclaimed and possibly begin to ask sufficient questions to understand the real nature of the disclaimer. Of course, such a theory assumes that consumers actually read documents presented to them when they are making a purchase. Although no research is available to provide exact numbers on whether consumers read such documents, many would suggest that consumer do not read such documents.

Disclaimers of implied warranties have specific rules and elements. It is easier to understand these rules by considering the implied warranty of merchantability and the implied warranty of fitness for a particular purpose separately.

The language of the Uniform Commercial Code seems to suggest that the disclaimer for the implied warranty for merchantability may be oral or may be written. The possibility of an oral disclaimer of merchantability should be considered first. As a practical matter, it is unlikely that an oral disclaimer of merchantability will be successful. First, the seller will find substantial proof problems on the matter of the facts. The buyer may deny having heard the disclaimer or disagree with the exact language of the disclaimer. As a fact problem, a jury would get to decide what was actually said. Most sellers would find it in their best interest to use a written disclaimer. In addition, there is the general problem of "Unconscionability." The U.C.C. allows the court to strike any language of a contract of sale that is unconscionable. An oral disclaimer that may have been misunderstood by the buyer will appear to be unconscionable. It appears, therefore, that most attempts to disclaim merchantability will be written.

For a written disclaimer of the implied warranty of merchantability, it must be conspicuous and mention the word merchantability. (It should be noted that even oral disclaimers of this implied warranty must mention the word merchantability.) The key problem is, therefore, one of conspicuousness. The language must be such so that reasonable person would have noticed it. In reviewing a disclaimer for whether it is conspicuous, the courts will look at a variety of issues. The courts will look at the location of the language in the document, the size of the type, the color of the type and the types of headings that introduce the disclaimer.

In order to disclaim the implied warranty of fitness for a particular purpose, the U.C.C. states specific elements. Unlike the disclaimer for merchantability, the U.C.C. states that the disclaimer for fitness must be in writing. Then, as with the disclaimer for merchantability, the disclaimer for fitness must be conspicuous. Finally, the U.C.C. gives an example of an adequate disclaimer for this warranty. It would be adequate to state, "There are no warranties which extend beyond the description on the face thereof."

The U.C.C. does provide additional material that explains how the disclaimers may be stated. (U.C.C. 2-316) The U.C.C. provides that the disclaimer may say, "as is," "with all faults," or such other language as would call to the attention of the buyer that the warranties are being disclaimed.

At one level it is obvious why such language should be sufficient. Most ordinary consumers would understand what "as is" means. Consumers have seen and used such language a sufficient number of times to understand that the sale is final and without recourse. There are, however, a few problems with even such disclaimers.

First, the "as is" disclaimer will not disclaim an express warranty. The special language protecting express warranties would find that "as is" disclaimer to be inconsistent with the express warranty. As such, the "as is" disclaimer would not be valid.

In addition, it would seem odd to find an "as is" disclaimer for the sale of a new product. An ordinary consumer could well be confused by such a disclaimer and it may not be valid. Such a disclaimer appears more often with the sale of used products.

As with all other disclaimers, the "as is" language must be conspicuous. Just because the U.C.C. provides for this type of disclaimer, that does not release the seller from the other requirements of the code.

Finally, the "as is" disclaimer would not relieve the seller from fraud. Attempts to stand behind such a broad disclaimer in order to avoid fraudulent behavior would not work.

After the reading the above material it is clear that sellers may disclaim all warranties. In order to do so, sellers would have to avoid making any express warranties and closely follow the language of the U.C.C. for disclaiming the implied warranties. Although all of the following detail might not be necessary to disclaim the warranties, an example of a complete disclaimer can be imagined.

The seller would want to place the disclaimer language on the front page of the sales contract. It would also be helpful to have a place for the buyer's signature with the disclaimer language so it can be proven that the language was seen. In order to make the language conspicuous is could be in a large font and in a different color of ink. The disclaimer language could be contained inside a box and have a heading in large type that said, "Disclaimer of All Warranties." The body of the disclaimer could then say, "All warranties, both express and implied are hereby disclaimed. There are no express warranties, no implied warranties of merchantability and no implied warranties of fitness for a particular purpose. There are no warranties which extend beyond the description of the face hereon. This product is being sold 'as is,' and 'with all faults.'"

Since that language would clearly disclaim all warranties, it raises an interesting question as to why more sellers fail to use such clear language. The reason has little to do with law and much to do with marketing. In a competitive consumer market, sellers do not want to scare off purchasers. An ordinary consumer who went into a department store to buy a toaster and saw a disclaimer like the one above, would probably go to a different store. Sellers want to avoid some liability, but also need to sell products. Because of this need to sell products, sellers tend to avoid using such strong language. In fact, sellers may allow warranties to exist with the product, but try to limit the extent of recovery that buyers may obtain. Such problems are discussed in the next section.

4. Limitation of Damages

A seller of goods may wish to extend express or implied warranties to a buyer, but also wish to limit the remedies that the buyer may seek in the event of a breach of one of those warranties. A fairly typical limitation of remedy to be found is the attempt to limit the buyer to repair or replacement of the goods in the event that a breach occurred. The Uniform Commercial Code allows for such limitations on remedies in U.C.C. 2-719.

In some settings this limitation on remedies appears to work. Back when people use to buy film for cameras, it was common for such rolls of film to carry a "repair or replacement" warranty. The warranty would guarantee that the film would work for ordinary picture taking. The box of film would actually contain language making such promises, but then go on to say that in the event the film had a defect, it should be returned to the manufacturer for a replacement roll of film. The language would also note that there were neither other warranties nor remedies to be allowed.

Using the film example, one can imagine the type of issues that could arise. A buyer might purchaser 10 rolls of film in preparation for attending a "once in a lifetime" family reunion. The buyer would then go on a long trip to return to the home of his or her youth. While at the family reunion, the buyer might take pictures of all family members including those going back three or four generations. The buyer might use all 10 rolls of film during the reunion and promise copies of pictures to everyone at the event. After returning from the reunion, the buyer might seek to have the film developed only to discover that the film was defective. None of the pictures would turn out. The film buyer might want to sue for substantial damages. There would be the cost of the trip, the lost time and effort, the broken promises to other family members and the pain and suffering due to lost opportunity since it would be impossible to ever get all of those family members together again. Assuming that the film carried the "repair or replacement" limitation of remedy, the courts would not allow those extensive damages. The buyer would only be able to recover replacement rolls of film.

The U.C.C. was drafted with the recognition that such a limitation of damages may not be appropriate in all cases. The U.C.C. notes that the limitation of remedy will not be enforced under some circumstances. "Where circumstances cause an exclusive or limited remedy to fail of its essential purpose, remedy may be had as provided in this act." U.C.C. 2-719(2). Basically, this means that where the warranty that was sought to be limited, "failed in its essential purpose," then the full range of remedies are allowed. It is, of course, necessary to determine what the code means with the "failed essential purpose" language.

Assume that a buyer purchases a new lawn mower for use at his or her home. The lawn mower may come with a 3 year warranty that states that the manufacturer will repair or replace any defects within that period. Again, the language may disclaim all other warranties and limit all other remedies. Then imagine that during the first summer of use, the lawn mower continues to fail to operate. Each time the buyer tries to cut his or her yard, the lawn mower shuts down. The buyer has to return the mower to the dealer for repairs. After about a week of repairs, the mower is picked up and used again. Before the buyer can finish cutting his or her yard, the mower fails. At some point, the buyer may want to sue for more than repair of the mower. The mower, and its warranty of service, has "failed it essential purpose." The essential purpose of the warranty was to provide a working lawn mower for three years. That is not occurring. The mower is staying at the repair shop rather than being used to mow. This is the type of circumstance where the limitation on remedy is probably invalid. The buyer could seek full recovery under the U.C.C.

The U.C.C. provides another method of holding limitations on remedies to be invalid. The U.C.C. specifically indicates that if the attempt to limit consequential damages is "unconscionable" then the limitation will not be enforced. U.C.C. 2-719(3). It also states that, "Limitation of consequential damages for injury to the person in the case of consumer goods is prima facie unconscionable but limitation of damages where the loss is commercial is not." U.C.C. 2-719(3). This special "unconscionability" section is obviously important in the typical products liability case.

An example of this provision can be imagined in a common type of case. Imagine that the purchaser needs to buy new tires for his or her automobile. Upon purchasing the tires, the buyer is given a 40,000 mile warranty for the tires. The warranty provides that the tires will be repaired or replaced if the tire tread is less than a specified amount within that 40,000 mile warranty. It also provides that road hazard flats will be repaired without cost. All other warranties are disclaimed and no other remedies will be allowed.

An accident could occur within the first 10,000, due to a defect in the tire where the tire blows out while the buyer is driving his or her car on the interstate. The blow out could cause a serious accident where the buyer is injured. If the buyer tried to recover for personal injuries due to the blow out, the manufacturer would claim that the remedies were limited to repair or replacement of the tire. The U.C.C. would find that this limitation that would prevent recovery for personal injury would be prima facie unconscionable. The courts would allow the buyer to use the 40,000 mile warranty to recover all for damages including the personal injury.

There should now appear to be some inconsistencies in the U.C.C. In the section on disclaimers, it was noted that the seller of goods could disclaim all warranties. If the seller was careful to use the precise words required by the U.C.C., then all of the warranties could be disclaimed. This discussion of limitations, however, raises the problem. Once the seller has created a warranty, limiting the recovery is difficult. In fact, it is prima facie unconscionable to try to limit recovery for personal injury for consumer goods. This apparent inconsistency is probably a result of the recognition that the ordinary consumer is not able to make fine, legal distinctions. There is a concern that if a consumer sees warranty language, the consumer may not understand that the warranty does not cover very much. On the other hand, if the consumer sees clear, concise disclaimer language, the consumer will be on notice that something is amiss in the transaction. This allows the seller to avoid liability if that seller wants to clearly disclaim warranties. If the seller wants to give some warranties, however, the seller can not use legal terms to limit the remedy to an extent that might not be noticed by the buyer.

One can imagine that this issue will continue to arise in the sale of consumer goods. Sellers are hesitant to use the clear, concise, conspicuous language of disclaimers that would avoid all liability. Such language would hurt sales in the marketplace. For that reason, sellers will continue to provide warranties. Lawyers for sellers, however, will continue to try to limit the liability of the clients. That will result in attempts to use limitation of remedy language. Litigation will continue on whether such language can be used in consumer goods transactions.

It is important to note that most of these issues arise with sales of consumer goods. Where the transaction is a commercial sale between businesses, there is an assumption that businesses will have teams of lawyers reading and analyzing the contracts. It is unlikely that a business transaction will confuse the parties. For that reason, the U.C.C. specifically notes that a limitation of consequential damage is not prima facie unconscionable where the loss is commercial. U.C.C. 2-719(3).

5. Unconscionability

The Uniform Commercial Code provides for the invalidation of contract provisions when such provisions are deemed unconscionable. Although that concept has broad application in the U.C.C., it will only arise in narrow settings in products liability cases. The typical example where unconscionability may arise in the products liability example is where the seller seeks to disclaim warranties or limit remedies.

The U.C.C. provides two sections that mention unconscionability. The general section, U.C.C. 2-302, indicates that any contract term may be invalidated it if is unconscionable. U.C.C. 2-719(3) is the specific section that deals with unconscionable attempts to limit remedies. The issues surrounding these topics were discussed in the section of this work immediately above.

6. Privity

Privity is an important concept in contract law. When two parties enter into a contract, that contract does not give some third party stranger the right to enforce provisions of the contract. (There are some narrow exceptions to that rule for third party beneficiary contracts, but they are not important to the discussion of products liability.) In the products liability setting, this would mean that when a product was defective, only those sellers in privity with the buyer could be responsible for breach of warranty. The Uniform Commercial Code deals with the issue of privity and expands the protections available to people injured by products.

Before fully discussing the issue of privity, the extent of the marketing chain must be understood. Because of the long marketing chain, the issue of privity can arise in two distinct ways. It is important to understand the difference between vertical and horizontal privity.

Vertical privity deals with the issue of those parties involved in manufacturing, marketing, and, ultimately, selling the product. The retail seller is the bottom of that marketing chain. Going up the vertical list, the next step would be the wholesaler. Continuing on up would take the vertical chain to the manufacturer. Of course, there may be others in that vertical marketing chain. Those would include, at a minimum, component part manufacturers. The question becomes whether a purchaser of the product from the retailer can also seek to recover for breach of warranty from those up that vertical chain? Obviously, the purchaser is in privity with the retail seller, but that same purchaser is not in privity with those other parties up that vertical chain.

Horizontal privity deals with those that are actually involved with purchasing and using the product. It would start, of course with the retailer seller. Extending horizontally out from the retail seller would be the purchaser as the first party. In the products liability setting, however, a case can frequently arise when someone other than the purchaser is injured. The horizontal privity chain may then extend from the purchaser to family members, guests, users, innocent bystanders, or other random third parties. The question with this issue is whether those, other than the purchaser, would have a claim for breach of warranty against the retail seller, or, for that matter, anyone else in the vertical chain.

Under traditional contract rules, no one would have an action unless they were in privity. As such, none of the third parties in the horizontal chain would have an action for breach of warranty. Only the purchaser was in privity with anyone and only that purchaser would have an action. The purchaser's action would be limited to only those with whom the purchaser was in privity. That would mean that the purchaser could only seek a breach of warranty action against the retail seller. Since the retailer seller was in privity with the wholesaler, the retail seller could, of course, sue the wholesaler. The wholesaler could then sue the manufacturer. Under the traditional rules, each party could only sue that party in privity.

The Uniform Commercial Code has specific language that deals with the issue of horizontal privity. U.C.C. 2-318 provides three alternative sections that states can adopt in dealing with this issue. Although Alternative A is the majority rule, each of the possible provisions must be noted.

Alternative A is the narrowest of the three possible provisions. This provision provides that "any natural person who is in the family or house hold of his buyer or who is a guest in his home," may recover. This obviously limits the actions available to a narrow range of plaintiffs. Those plaintiffs who may be bystanders, for example, would not be allowed to sue for breach of warranty. An interesting problem arises with employees. A substantial number of products liability cases arise in the work place setting. An employee is injured, recovers workers' compensation from the employer and then seeks to sue the manufacturer of the equipment that caused the injured. If the state has adopted the alternative A, the employee does not look like a member of the family, house hold or guest. This issue has caused some split of authority. Some jurisdictions have been inclined to extend the meaning of house hold to include people such as employees. Other jurisdictions have taken a more literal approach to the language and refused such expansion.

Alternative A has another limitation that is implied by the language. That alternative indicates that the plaintiff must have been injured "in person." This language has led courts to indicate that those plaintiffs, other than one in strict privity, are limited to recovery for personal injury. Those other plaintiffs who may sue under alternative A may not sue for property damage or economic loss.

Alternative B to U.C.C. 2-318 is broader than alternative A. This alternative indicates that plaintiffs may include "any natural person who may be reasonably expected" to use the product. This extends the possible plaintiffs to something like the tort theory of foreseeable plaintiffs. This would allow the innocent bystanders of products to sue for breach of warranty. Like alternative A, however, alternative B limits actions to one "who is injured in person." This language has allowed courts to limit recovery to personal injury. Unless the plaintiff is in privity with the seller, the plaintiff cannot sue for property damage or economic losses under alternative B.

Alternative C is the broadest of the three available sections. This alternative allows recover for breach of warranty by "any person who may be reasonably expected to use" the product. In addition, alternative C does not contain the limitation to injuries to the person. This alternative, therefore, would allow recovery by any foreseeable person for any foreseeable injury.

The issue of vertical privity under the Uniform Commercial Code is less clear. The U.C.C. does not have a specific provision that deals with vertical privity. Keep in mind that under the U.C.C. the plaintiff must be included in the appropriate alternative to U.C.C. 2-318. If, for example, a state has adopted alternative A and a bystander wants to bring an action, that bystander does not have a claim for breach of warranty. If, however, members of the family or house hold wants to sue, that plaintiff may sue in a state with alternative A. That, however, does not answer the question of whether that party may sue someone other than the retailer seller.

The first issue to consider when looking at liability of those in the vertical chain of distribution is the problem of express warranties. It is not uncommon for manufacturers to prepare advertisements, brochures, or other publicly announced statements. A buyer may well rely upon those statements when making a purchase from the retailer seller. If the buyer wants to sue the manufacturer for those express warranties, the manufacturer will claim that there is no privity between the manufacturer and the buyer. Although that would have limited the claim in the past, most jurisdictions have abolished the need for privity up the vertical chain for express warranties. If a prospective defendant made affirmations of fact that were part of the basis of the bargain, then that defendant may be liable for the express warranty even if that defendant was not in privity with the buyer.

Implied warranties have not been so broadly extended. There is a split of authority on this issue. Some jurisdictions have abolished the need for vertical privity for implied warranty claims, while others have not. Even some states that have abolished the need for privity for express warranty claims continue to require it for implied warranty claims.

Privity, therefore, remains a difficult issue for warranty claims. The available of alternative sections for horizontal privity and the absence of any clear language on vertical privity leaves the issue substantially non-uniform. The issue must be researched in each jurisdiction to determine how it will be handled in that location.

Warranty Checkpoints

- There are three types of warranties:

  - Express warranty
  - Implied warranty of fitness for a particular purpose
  - Implied warranty of merchantability

- The express warranty requires:

  - An affirmation of fact or promise that is a basis of the bargain; or
  - A sale by sample that is a basis of the bargain; or
  - A sale by description that is a basis of the bargain.

- The implied warranty of fitness for a particular purpose requires:

  - That the seller know of the specific purpose that the buyer intends for the product; and
  - That the buyer relies upon the expertise of the seller in selecting the product.

- The implied warranty of merchantability requires:

  - A merchant seller; and
  - A product fails to be adequate for ordinary purposes.

Chapter 5

Misrepresentation

Misrepresentation Roadmap

- Understand general elements of a claim for misrepresentation
- Distinguish intent, negligence and strict liability in a misrepresentation claim

---

A. Elements of the Claim

1. General Elements

Misrepresentation has been a claim for a long period of time. It may be referred to by a series of different names in different jurisdictions. Whether it goes by the name of fraud, deceit, or misrepresentation, it has similar elements that must be met.

Although it has been used for a series of different types of claims, it has become one of the available remedies for a products liability claim. Where the seller makes false representations about a product, a failure of a product to perform as claimed can lead to liability. As such, it appears to be very similar to the contract remedy of express warranty.

There are, of course, differences between the remedies of misrepresentation and warranty. As discussed in the section on warranty, express warranty is a contract like claim that is governed by the Uniform Commercial Code. Under the U.C.C., express warranty claims may require notice and have some issues related to the problem of privity. Disclaimers and limitations of remedies may also generate some difficulties with the claim for express warranty. Since misrepresentation is a tort claim, the issues of notice, privity, disclaimer, and limitation of remedies do not arise. It is common for plaintiffs' lawyers to include claims for express warranty and misrepresentation together. Although they are both based on false statements, the various other elements leads the lawyers to claim both in an effort to make sure some claim gets to a jury.

The basic elements of misrepresentation in a product claim are the same as for any other misrepresentation. Although those elements may be stated in different ways, an easy statement of the elements may be as follows:

1. A false representation of a material fact; and
2. Basis of liability (sometimes called scienter); and
3. Intent to induce reliance; and
4. Justifiable reliance; and
5. Damages.

Each of these elements will be more fully discussed in the following material of this chapter. The most difficult issue is the one concerning basis of liability. In products liability cases, the misrepresentation claim may be based on intent, negligence or strict liability.

2. False Representation of a Material Fact

The first element of an action for misrepresentation requires that there be a false representation of a material fact. Ordinarily, this element should present no difficult. If the seller has made oral or written assertions concerning the product, those are representations. It may also be considered a representation when the seller provides pictures or descriptions of the product. The difficulty can arise when the buyer seeks to hold the seller for failing to inform of problems.

Usually, there is no duty to disclose. This allows a seller to remain silent and avoid liability for misrepresentation. There are, however, some exceptions to the "no duty to disclose" rule. Where there is a partial statement, the seller has a duty to fully explain. If a partial statement leaves the buyer with confusion or a wrong impression concerning the product, then an action will lie. In addition, if the seller makes positives steps to conceal difficulties or defects with the product, the courts may find that sufficient for a misrepresentation action. The attempt to actively conceal such problems will be actionable. Finally, the failure to disclose information may give rise to other types of actions. The failure to fully explain risks associated with the product may avoid liability for misrepresentation while subjecting the seller to an action for failure to warn.

In seeking to recover for misrepresentation, the false representation must have been of a fact. As with warranty claims, statements that appear to be opinion or sales puffing will not be actionable.

3. Scienter or Basis of Liability

The element that concerns the basis of liability may be the most complex. A misrepresentation for a product claim may, in fact, be based on any basis of liability. The action may be brought in intent, negligence or strict liability.

The intentional falsehood subjects the seller to an action for fraud. In order to prove this type of misrepresentation, the plaintiff must prove that the seller knew the statement was false, made the statement without belief in the truth, or made the statement in reckless disregard of the truth.

The importance of trying to prove intent rather than merely relying on one of the other basis is the available damages. If the plaintiff is able to prove that the seller knew the statements were false when they were made, then, in addition to compensatory damages, punitive damages may be available.

If the plaintiff is unable to prove that the seller knew the statements were false when they were made, the plaintiff may seek to recover for negligent misrepresentation. This basis requires that the plaintiff can show that the seller failed to use reasonable care to discover the truth before making the representation.

The final basis of misrepresentation is strict liability. The Restatement (Second) of Torts § 402B provides for this basis of liability. This provisions allows for strict liability but adds some special requirements of proof. The seller may be liable for the false statement even though it was an innocent falsehood. Such an action would lie even though the seller did not know the statement was false and no reasonable seller would have known the statement was false. To recover, however, the plaintiff must prove the additional elements.

First, in order to recover for the strict liability misrepresentation, the defendant must have been in the business of selling such products. This is very much like the requirement of business seller found in Restatement (Second) of Torts § 402A. The casual seller or non business seller cannot be held liable for the strict liability misrepresentation.

In addition, the seller held liable for strict liability misrepresentation may only be held liable for damages due to physical harm to the person or property of the plaintiff. The plaintiff cannot recover pure economic loss and that includes the reduced value of the product itself.

The action for strict liability misrepresentation looks much like an action for express warranty under the Uniform Commercial Code. The damages issue, of course, is one of the major differences. Where the misrepresentation claim is limited to physical harm damages, the express warranty claim allows recovery for economic losses.

4. Intent to Induce Reliance

The next element adds an intent requirement to all misrepresentation actions. In order for the plaintiff to recover, there must be proof that the seller intended to induce reliance on the part of the plaintiff. This would require that the seller was speaking for the purpose of having an influence on the plaintiff in either the purchase or use of the product.

This element seems to work closely with three other parts of the action. In order to recover the representation must have been of a "material" fact and the reliance on the representation must have been justified. In some ways, those two elements along with the requirement of intent to induce reliance work together. All three seem to be working to require that the representation was of sufficient importance in the eyes of both the seller and the plaintiff that the plaintiff felt the representation was an important part of the reason to purchase and use the product.

This element seems to be similar to a part of express warranty. In the discussion of express warranty, it was noted that the warranty had to be part of the basis of the bargain. In other words, the warranty needed to be influential in the purchase or use of the product. Without using the phrase, "basis of the bargain," the action for misrepresentation requires much the same element.

5. Justifiable Reliance

Proof of justifiable reliance is also important to the plaintiff's case. It is not every misrepresentation that gives rise to a claim. The representation must have been important to the plaintiff. If the plaintiff purchased or used the product based upon his or her own thoughts or opinion, then no action will lie for the fact that the defendant made a false statement.

The reliance must have also been justified. This requires that it be the type of reliance that one would find reasonable people engaging in. If the plaintiff claims to have relied on outrageous opinions or sales puffing, the courts will not allow the action. The reliance must have been justified.

6. Damages

Misrepresentation is a tort and, as such, should be governed by the rules of damages that apply to tort law. Misrepresentation, however, is not so limited. The available damages for an action in misrepresentation depend on the basis of liability for the claim.

Fraudulent or intentional misrepresentations require a showing that the defendant knew the statement was false when it was made. This claim allow the plaintiff to recover for personal injury, property damage and some economic losses. Although economic losses are ordinarily not available in tort claims, misrepresentation has traditionally allowed such claims. The plaintiff should be able to recover such claims including the loss of value of the product itself.

The major benefit of an intentional misrepresentation, however, is the availability of punitive damages. Since the defendant will have acted intentionally or recklessly, the plaintiff will be entitled to such exemplary damages.

Negligent misrepresentation allows recovery for the typical negligence damages. Those include personal injury and property damages. As a form of misrepresentation, the plaintiff will also be able to recover for the loss of value of the product. Punitive damages are, of course, not recoverable for negligent misrepresentation.

Strict liability misrepresentation has been discussed above. The plaintiff may recover for personal injury or property damage. The plaintiff may not recover for economic losses nor for punitive damages.

B. Important Distinctions between Misrepresentation and Express Warranty

The tort action for misrepresentation is very similar to the contract/Uniform Commercial Code action for breach of express warranty. It is important to note some of the critical differences.

1. Notice

Warranties under the Uniform Commercial Code require that the plaintiff give notice of defect or deficiency to the defendant at a reasonable time. For the consumer product user, this requirement has been a problem for seeking recovery for warranty claims. Consumers rarely understand the necessity of giving notice. In fact, consumers usually do not give notice until they seek advice of counsel and the attorney provides notice.

Misrepresentation claims do not require the giving of notice. They are, of course, bound by statutes of limitations. If, however, the action was brought within the required limitation period, the absence of prior notice will not defeat the claim.

2. Disclaimers

The Uniform Commercial Code provides for the availability of disclaimers for warranty claims. As discussed in the chapter on warranties, it is difficult to disclaim an express warranty. That issue, however, does not arise in a misrepresentation claim. There is no defense of disclaimer in misrepresentation.

3. Limitations of Remedies

Although disclaiming express warranties under the Uniform Commercial Code is difficult, it is possible to limit the available remedies under the code. Misrepresentation actions, however, are not governed by the code. Misrepresentation actions may not have the remedies limited by the seller.

4. Basis of Liability

Express warranty actions are in the nature of strict liability. There is no requirement of proof of intent or negligence in seeking to recover for express warranty. Misrepresentation actions allow recovery in intent, negligence and strict liability. Although strict liability would appear to be the easiest claim for the plaintiff to seek, there may be reasons that the plaintiff would prefer intent or negligence. Intent and negligence may allow some recovery for economic losses while intentional actions will also allow recovery for punitive damages.

5. Damages

As discussed throughout this chapter, the issue of damages remains a major issue in misrepresentation and warranty. The action for express warranty allows recovery for personal injury, property damage, and economic loss. Although actions for intentional and negligent misrepresentation also allow such recoveries, strict liability misrepresentation is more limited. No recovery for economic loss is allowed for the strict liability misrepresentation. It must also be noted that, unlike any of the other claims, intentional misrepresentation allows recovery for punitive damages.

Misrepresentation Checkpoints

- The basic elements of misrepresentation are:
    - False representation of a material fact; and
    - Scienter or basis of liability; and
    - The intent to induce reliance; and
    - Justifiable reliance; and
    - Damages.
- The three bases of liability in misrepresentation are:
    - Intent; or
    - Negligence; or
    - Strict liability.

Chapter 6

Parties

One of the major issues in a product's liability action is who the proper parties to the litigation are. A products liability action may be based on tort, contract and several different bases of liability. In addition, the modern chain of distribution is long and global in scope. A plaintiff may want to bring in multiple defendants just to make sure someone is ultimately liable and able to pay a judgment. It is also true that the buyer may not be the injured party. A bystander may want to sue for injuries received from a defective product. With all of those variables, the identity of the proper parties will depend on the nature of the specific action.

A. Plaintiff

The first issue that must be addressed in most product actions is the proper plaintiff. As discussed in Chapter 1, privity use to be a major issue. In the 1800's, a plaintiff could not sue for injuries due to a defective product unless that plaintiff was in privity with the seller. The privity rule applied to actions in tort and actions in contract. In the early 1900's, the privity rule was abolished for tort actions. More recent changes in the Uniform Commercial Code have also relaxed the requirement of privity for actions for breach of warranty.

In modern tort actions, there is no longer a requirement of privity. The current tradition in negligence claims is to limit the proper plaintiff to a "foreseeable plaintiff." That term is somewhat vague, but does provide the guidelines for identifying the plaintiff. Some courts may state it is as being a plaintiff that a reasonable person ought to have been able to foresee. It should be obvious that a buyer of a product will be a foreseeable plaintiff. In addition, courts have determined that family members, close relations, users and even bystanders come within the range of foreseeable plaintiff. Although some cases may require review of the facts on a case by case basis, the range of possible plaintiffs is large.

With the adoption of strict liability under Restatement (Second) of Torts § 402A, the question of proper plaintiff also arose for such actions. That section of the restatement indicates that the plaintiff includes "users and consumers." That phrase has been interpreted broadly by the courts. It has included buyers, users, and bystanders. In many ways, the phrase "foreseeable plaintiff" seems to be the same concept as "users or consumers."

Actions for breach of warranty under the Uniform Commercial Code are governed by that code. The code provides a specific provision for dealing with the identity of the proper plaintiff for an action for breach of warranty. U.C.C. 2-318 provides for three alternative options that states may adopt. Alternative A is the most restrict and limits the proper plaintiff to the buyer, family member or guest in the household. This alternative is the majority in the United States. Alternative B is broader and extends to any natural person for personal injuries. Alternative C extends to any person for any injury.

It must be kept in mind that merely because a person finds him or herself injured and within the group of proper plaintiffs does not guarantee a recovery. In an action for negligence, for example, the foreseeable plaintiff must still prove all of the elements of negligence. In an action for strict liability, the "user or consumer" must also prove all of the elements of strict liability. Warranty claims are even more difficult. Although the implied warranty of merchantability appears similar to strict liability in tort, the express warranty requires that the warranty be the basis of the bargain. An injured party who never heard the warranty would not be able to recover for express warranty even though that person may have been within the terms of the proper plaintiff section adopted in that jurisdiction. The implied warranty of fitness for a particular purpose has much the same problem. Even though a plaintiff is within the terms of U.C.C. 2-318, they must have relied upon the expertise of the seller in order to recover for that warranty.

In short, the decision as to the proper plaintiff is an important element of any products liability action. It is, however, only one element. Care must be used to make sure all of elements of any alleged claim are met.

B. Seller

Once it is determined who is the proper plaintiff, determining whether a defendant may be kept in the litigation must also be discussed. Dating back to the period when privity was required, the immediate seller would have always have been a proper defendant. If the buyer had purchased a product from the person who made it, then there would not have been a problem with parties. The buyer and seller would have been in privity and there would not have been any other possible defendants. Prior to the industrial revolution, that would have been a possibility. A buyer who wanted a wagon, a saddle or some other home use product, would have probably purchased it from the person who made it. Clearly such a situation rarely exists today. There may be times when a buyer will purchase a handmade craft object directly from the person who made it, but most products do not fit within that situation today.

Most products today are the result of a long chain of distribution. Component part manufactures may create small parts that will be used in large products. Such component part manufactures may be the makers of steel that ultimately goes into automobiles, they may be the farmers that grow wheat for bread, or they may be the manufactures of wire that will be used as heating elements for toasters. Manufacturers in many cases today may more appropriately be called final assemblers. They do not manufacture from raw materials; they, instead, assemble a finished product from a group of component parts. Those manufactures rarely sell directly to consumers. Instead, many manufacturers deal through wholesalers. Those wholesalers also do not deal directly with consumers. Many of the wholesalers purchases products and resell them through retailers. In fact, there are times that the wholesaler may not even have contact with the product that is being sold. The wholesaler may purchase the product and resell it to a retailer without having to take possession of the product. The wholesaler may just have the product shipped directly from the manufacturer to the retailers. Retailers are the ones who ultimately sell it to the consumer.

In the simple times of the 1800s, the consumer could sue the retailer, but no one else. During that time, the retailer was, frequently, the manufacturer and the only one with whom the buyer had any dealings. Limiting recovery as only between those two made sense during that period. In the modern word of global markets and long chains of distribution, the limitation of recovery as only between those two no longer makes sense.

C. Chain of Distribution

As noted above, the modern distribution of products is the result of a long and, frequently, global market. Manufacturers buy component parts from all over the world. Products are assembled by manufacturers and shipped all over the world through wholesalers. Wholesalers deliver products to retailers for final sale to consumers.

Although the sale from the retailer to the consumer appears to be the "final" sale, that is not really so. Even during the distribution of the product when it is new, there are other people involved in that distribution. Sellers along the way may own the franchise to sell the product that they did not personally make. Some sellers may be buying products and putting their own names on it. In the modern era of celebrities, there may be people endorsing products to encourage the purchase and use of those products. Also, while the product is moving through the chain of distribution, corporations involved in that chain may merge, go out of business, or reopen under a different name. All of those parties may be sought out as defendants when a consumer is injured by a product.

The discussion of the chain of distribution only assumed the existence of "new" products. Obviously, many products last long enough to enter a secondary marketing chain. Automobiles, for example, are frequently traded in or resold as used products. That raises the issue of whether dealers of used products ought to be liable in the same way as new product sellers.

Finally, there are a variety of different types of transactions that injured plaintiffs have attempted to make appear sufficiently like products liability in order to use strict liability in the case. Real estate transactions, leases, and the delivery of services are examples of those recurring problems.

All of the above possible defendants raise problems in the products liability area. All of them will be discussed below. There are a few issues, however, that may be discussed about those possible defendants as a general matter.

As noted in the discussion about possible plaintiffs, the issue for plaintiffs in tort cases is whether the plaintiff is a "foreseeable plaintiff." Regardless of who in the chain of distribution was sued, the only question is whether the plaintiff was "foreseeable" to that defendant. Any defendant from the component part manufacturer to the retailer may have been able to "foresee" the plaintiff. As such, any of the defendants may be included within the litigation.

Issues of warranty are more difficult. The Uniform Commercial Code has a specific section to cover the possible plaintiffs. That issue, known as horizontal privity, is covered in U.C.C. 2-318 and was discussed above. The issue of who may be held liable up the chain of distribution, known as vertical privity, does not have a specific U.C.C. section. This has left states to determine exactly what to do with the question when confronted with it. Some states have taken a strict privity approach and require privity between the defendant and those parties noted in the special section dealing with the proper plaintiffs. This would require a proper plaintiff to sue a retailer and then the retailer to sue any wholesaler. The wholesaler could then sue a manufacturer. Other jurisdictions have assumed the absence of a section removed the privity requirement. In such jurisdictions, proper plaintiffs identified in U.C.C. 2-318 have been allowed to sue anyone up the chain of distribution.

Keep in mind, however, that the issue is not as simple as that brief, general discussion would suggest. That is just an introductory note to the more complex problem. The remainder of this chapter will discuss the details of the issue.

D. Manufacturer, Wholesaler, Retailer, Component Part Manufacturer

The first, and most obvious possible defendants, are those parties in the initial chain of distribution. The possibility of including the component part manufacturer, manufacturer, wholesaler and retailer in a products liability action as a defendant will depend on the nature of the legal claim being brought and the facts.

1. Component Part Manufacturers

Component part manufacturers are at the very beginning of the marketing chain. They may include those that supply raw materials for the ultimate product like the producers of steel that will ultimately become automobiles. They may also include parties who make small parts that are added to larger parts for a finished product. That would include the company that makes batteries for installation into new cars on the assembly line. None of these component part manufacturers are automatically excluded from liability. It is important, however, to consider the facts and circumstance of each type of case to determine whether those possible defendants may be held liable.

Issues concerning warranty and component part manufacturers may be the easiest to understand. Such defendants may be held liable, but they must have breached a warranty. Rarely, for example, will a component part manufacturer extend an express warranty to an ultimate purchaser. Usually the component part is included in a larger product and the final assembler will provide any warranties. Imagine, for example, the producer of the steel that is manufactured into an automobile. There is little likelihood that the steel manufacturer extended an express warranty. It is also unlikely that the steel manufacturer participated in the purchase by a consumer and extended an implied warranty of fitness for a particular purpose.

There are examples, however, where an express warranty may be extended by a component part manufacturer. The manufacturer of automobile tires that are installed on a new car before delivery to the dealership usually provides a warranty. This warranty is usually for a specific term and limits liability to repair or replacement of the tire. Should the tire fail in a way that breaches the warranty, the tire manufacturer would be a defendant facing all of the issues discussed in the chapter on warranty.

A component part manufacturer may also have some issues with the implied warranty of merchantability. If a component part manufacture produces a product that does not meet the test of merchantability, then that defendant may be held liable for the implied warranty. Notice, however, how the facts of the case may create difficult issues.

A manufacturer of steel that supplies that steel to automobile manufacturers is a component part manufacturer. If an automobile has a frame produced from that steel, questions could arise if the frame broke during use and caused an injury producing wreck. The plaintiff may wish to sue the steel producer as well as the automobile manufacturer. The question would be whether the steel was actually not merchantable. The accident, for example, may have occurred for one of two different reasons. The steel may have been defective by having too many flaws, or the steel may have been fine while the frame was of a poor design that failed after short use. If the accident was due to defects in the original steel, the steel manufacturer would have breached an implied warranty of merchantability. If the frame design was the cause of the accident, the steel manufacturer may not have breached the warranty.

Strict liability cases in tort against component part manufacturers would be analyzed in much the same was as implied warranty of merchantability cases. The question would be whether the defect was in the component part when it left the component part manufacturer. If the defect was in the component part and that was the cause of the injury, then the component part manufacturer could be liable for strict liability in tort. If, however, the component part was not defective, but the accident was the result of the misapplication of the component part by a subsequent manufacturer of a larger product, then the component part manufacturer would not be liable for strict liability.

It is interesting that some jurisdictions analyze the issue with slightly different emphasis. Since the strict liability actions require that the product reach the consumer "without substantial change," some jurisdictions use that language to reach the same result. Using our steel example, such jurisdictions confronted with a faulty frame design would say that the steel underwent substantial change and strict liability would not apply. If the steel was defective, the jurisdiction could say that the defect was in the steel when it left the component part manufacturer and that defect was not changed.

Negligence cases against component part manufacturers would be analyzed in much the same way as strict liability cases. The question would be whether the part manufacturer failed to use reasonable care in the manufacturing of that part.

2. Manufacturers

After the discussion of component part manufacturers, the issue concerning the primary manufacturer should be simple. Placing the responsibility for the cost of injuries against the party most able to bear the loss and correct for future injuries has been the primary goals of products liability. Those goals can best be reached by placing liability on the primary manufacturer.

For actions in warranty, the question is always whether the manufacturer breached a warranty. With the sale of many new products, the manufacturer will extend an express warranty. Those warranties are enforceable against that manufacturer. Examples are easy to imagine. When a consumer purchases a new toaster, it may come with a 1 year express warranty. The warranty may, in fact, state that the product must be returned to the manufacturer for warranty work. The problem with many of these express warranties is that the manufacturer will attempt to limit the remedy to a repair or replacement remedy and exclude all other remedies. That would raise all of the issues already discussed in the chapter on warranties.

It is unlikely that a manufacturer will be held to an implied warranty of fitness for a particular purpose. Since the consumer did not deal directly with the manufacturer, there is little likelihood that the consumer relied upon the manufacturer for the selection of the product

Manufacturers may be held to implied warranties for merchantability. That implied warranty is thought to "run with the product." If the product proves to be not merchantable and that defect was in the product when it was produced, then there is a breach of the warranty.

Strict liability in tort is an obvious claim against manufacturers. As noted earlier, some of the purposes of strict liability were to place the cost of injury against the party best able to bear it and encourage the manufacturer to make safer products. If the product appears to have a defect and that defect was in the product when it left the manufacturer, then strict liability in tort is an appropriate remedy against the manufacturer

Negligence can be used against manufacturers, but contain all the difficulties of a negligence action. Proving that the manufacturer failed to use reasonable care is difficult and expensive for the plaintiff in preparation of the case. Although negligence is an allowable claim against the manufacturer, proving the case is difficult.

3. Wholesalers

Wholesalers, like manufacturers, are legally responsible under most of the possible products liability claims. Unlike manufacturers, however, the facts of the cases usually allow the wholesalers to avoid liability.

In cases of express warranty or the implied warranty of fitness for particular purpose, the wholesaler could be liable for such claims if the facts showed that the warranties were made and breached. Wholesalers rarely make express warranties. In addition, consumers rarely rely upon the expertise of the wholesaler in selecting the product in order to claim the implied warranty of fitness. In fact, consumers rarely know who the wholesaler was. As such, actions for express warranty and the implied warranty of merchantability against wholesalers are rare.

The implied warranty of merchantability creates and interesting problem for wholesalers. Since the warranty is held to "run with the product," the wholesaler may find that they have breached this warranty. If the defect was in the product when it was made by the manufacturer, then it was still in the product when it passed through the wholesaler to the retailer. This would mean that the wholesaler was a merchant who sold a product that was not merchantable. A wholesaler, therefore, may find a greater likelihood of being held liable for the implied warranty of merchantability.

Strict liability in tort may be an action against wholesalers. This claim would work much like the implied warranty of merchantability. If the defect was in the product when it left the manufacturer, the strict liability may attach to the wholesaler. The wholesaler is in the business of selling such products and sold a product in a defective condition unreasonably dangerous. Liability would apply.

Negligence is a possible claim against wholesalers, but would be rarely successful. In order to recover for negligence it is necessary to prove that the party failed to use reasonable care. Typically, wholesalers buy products in bulk and then ship them to retailers. In fact, wholesalers will frequently have the products shipped directly from the manufacturer to the retailer. The wholesaler will, in those cases, never see the product. Since the wholesaler does not make the product, it would be necessary to prove that the wholesaler failed to use reasonable care to inspect the product and find defects. Since the wholesaler has such little contact with the product, the duty to inspect is not realistic. Imagine, for example, a wholesaler of groceries. The wholesaler buys cases of cans of peas for further sale and shipment to a grocery store. If a consumer ultimately buys a can of peas from the grocery store and injures a tooth by biting down on a small stone in the peas, an action against the wholesaler for negligence would not be possible. In order for the wholesaler to know about the stone in the can of peas, the wholesaler would have had to open every case and then open every can of peas in order to inspect them. Not only is such an expected duty not "reasonable," it would be absurd. In order for the national marketing of products to take place, wholesalers cannot be expected to open and inspect every product.

4. Retailers

Retailers are most likely defendants in products liability actions. They are the party with whom the consumer had most direct contact, and retailers are most likely the one subject to all of the claims.

Even in jurisdictions that retain some vestige of a privity requirement for the vertical privity issue, the retailer is in privity with the buyer or consumer. As long as the plaintiff meets the terms of the alternative selected for U.C.C.2-318, then the retailer is a proper defendant. As such, the retailer could be sued for breach of express warranty or breach of either of the implied warranties. It would be required, of course, for the plaintiff to prove the elements of those claims, but there would be no automatic exclusion of the retailer from exposure to liability for the warranty actions.

Retailers can also be held liable for strict liability in tort. Retailers are in the business of selling such products. In addition, even though the retailer did not create the defect, the defect was in the product when it was sold by the retailer. Retailers, much like manufacturers are the primary defendants in strict liability claims.

Retailers may also be sued for negligence, but the facts of such cases make them difficult for plaintiffs. In order to hold a retailer liable for negligence, it will usually be necessary to show that the retailer failed to use reasonable care to inspect and find a defect. Such proof is difficult. Much like wholesalers, a retailer's duty to inspect is not great. Considering still the sale of peas by a grocery, it would not be reasonable to expect a grocery to inspect every can of peas by opening them. That would, of course, destroy the product. A retailer may have some greater duty to inspect, however, than a wholesaler. Where it is clear that a product is defective and the retailer chose not to notice, there could be a claim for negligence. The difficult part for the plaintiff would be to show the duty to inspect and the failure to use reasonable care to find the defect.

5. Additional Issues with the Initial Chain of Distribution

Within actions against the primary chain of distribution parties, a few additional issues have arisen. These seem to be small issues, but arise with sufficient regularity to require noting.

Some sellers of products place their own names on the product although they did not manufacturer them. It is easy to imagine the existence of generic products that carry the name of a large retailer. Relatively early in the development of products liability law, some such defendants sought to avoid liability by claiming they were not the manufacturers of such products. The courts were not sympathetic to that claim. By placing their name on the product, the sellers took responsibility for the quality of the product.

In more recent years, some state legislatures have sought to provide protections for some of the parties in the chain of distribution. Noting that the purpose of different forms of strict liability was to force manufacturers to pay the cost of injuries and encourage such manufacturers to improve products, some legislatures thought it would be appropriate to limit strict liability recover to only the manufacturers. A minority of states have passed legislation that, where the manufacturer is identified, all others in the chain of distribution are released from liability for strict liability in tort and the implied warranty of merchantability. Most of this legislation does allow actions against the others in the chain of distribution for such things as express warranty or negligence. Such legislation has the effect of protecting wholesalers and retailers from strict liability while putting the greatest risk of liability on the manufacturer.

E. Used Product

Used products have created a difficult issue for products liability law. Many products last long enough to move into a used product market. Used product buyers have sought to hold used product dealers liable when injuries have occurred. If a product was defective when it left the original manufacturer, then it is possible for the used product buyer to hold the original manufacturer liable in strict liability in tort. Negligence is also a viable claim. The warranty claims are less likely because of the limitations of extension of liability to remote users found under U.C.C. 2-318. All of those issues would be dealt with in the same manner as the discussion above concerning manufactures found in section D of this chapter. The more difficult issue is can the used product dealer be liable for defective products.

Courts have been willing to hold most used product dealers liable in negligence. That basis of liability is generally available and may be appropriate for this type of claim. The difficulty, of course, is proving the negligence claim. Courts are reluctant to impose a high duty on used product dealers, and plaintiffs find it difficult to prove the breach of reasonable care. Under those circumstances, used product dealers may be sued for negligence, but are rarely found liable.

Used product dealers are rarely included in a strict liability claim. Courts assume that strict liability was designed to impose liability on those most able to correct the defects in the products. It is assumed that used product dealers are outside the normal chain of distribution and would have little claim against the original manufacturer. Since the claim against the used product dealer would be inconsistent with the purposes of strict liability in tort, most courts deny that liability.

Noting that courts are concerned with the purposes of strict liability when considering such issues, several types of cases have imposed liability for strict liability on used product dealers. Where the product appears to have a long useful life, there is a traditional used market for such products, and there is the expectation that buyers will expect used products to continue to serve for an extended period, courts have applied strict liability. These cases are limited and can be easily understood. One example is the used sale of over the road trucks. The large trucks that are seen regularly on the highways are expected to last for an extended period. Many will be driven for 200,000 to 400,000 miles. Many of those truck engines are rebuilt on regular occasions and sold through the used product market. Some dealers sell heavily in that market. A few courts have determined that those facts make the sale of such trucks appropriate for strict liability. Outside of those few exceptional cases, used product dealers are not liable in strict liability in tort.

Used product dealers are rarely liable in warranty. Such dealers could be held for express warranty, but most such dealers do not give express warranties. The same is true of the warranty of fitness for a particular purpose. They could be held under such an implied warranty, but most avoid giving advice on selection of products. Courts have been reluctant to impose liability on used product dealers for the implied warranty of merchantability. Used products do not appear to be appropriate for claims under that basis.

In short, the most likely claim for a plaintiff's action against a used product dealer will be negligence. Even those claims, however, will be difficult for the plaintiff to win.

F. Successor Corporation

In the modern world of corporations, few corporations remain as a consistent entity for a long period of time. Problems arise in the products liability area when corporate manufacturers or sellers change their identity.

It should be clear that there are some easy examples to understand. If a corporate manufacturer or seller goes out of business that corporation is no longer liable. There is no longer an entity that can be sued. The prior stock holders in that corporation also cannot be sued. The purpose of corporations is to limit liability. It would only be under extreme examples of fraud that a plaintiff could "pierce the corporate veil" and sue a stockholder. Corporations, however, rarely just go out of business and disappear. Usually a corporation will be sold or merged into another corporation. The plaintiff will usually seek to recover against the new corporation that absorbed the older corporation.

The problems with successor corporations arise in products liability in a consistent manner. A corporation will be a manufacturer or seller of a product. The plaintiff will purchase the product and subsequently be injured by it. When the plaintiff seeks recover for injuries, it is discovered that the original corporation is no longer in existence, but has in some way been taken over by another corporation. When the plaintiff sues the new corporation, there is a general rule. That general rule is that the new corporation is not liable for the claims against the old corporation. The reason for the rule is obvious. Public policy encourages organizations to merge, combine, grow and continue to move the economy forward. If there was a fear of outstanding lawsuits, one corporation would never purchase another.

Although the general rule is that there is no liability of the successor corporation for conduct of the prior corporation, there are exceptions to the rule. Those exceptions have been developed through several court decisions and are generally recognized. Those exceptions are:

1. When the successor corporation expressly or impliedly assumes those prior liabilities; or

2. When the transaction was actually a consolidation or merger of the two corporations; or

3. When the purchasing corporation is a mere continuation of the former corporation; or

4. When there is a fraudulent intent to avoid liability.

Those four exceptions are the ones that are generally recognized in the United States. A few courts have expressed the desire to create another exception. It is worth noting, but it has not been adopted by all jurisdictions. A few jurisdictions have adopted an exception known as the "product line" exception. Imagine, for example, that the successor corporation buys a previous corporation and completely absorbs it. There are none of the four traditional exceptions that apply. Also imagine, however, that the new corporation continues to manufacture and sell a product that the older corporation had been producing. It would be easy to see that this could be the product that the plaintiff was injured by. The plaintiff would claim that the older corporation manufactured the specific item that caused his or her injuries, but the new corporation continues to manufacture the same items. As noted, a few courts have allowed that action to proceed. Again, however, that exception has not gained the support of a majority of jurisdictions.

G. Franchisor, Endorser

There are numerous methods of organizing a chain of distribution in the modern economy. Although the chain from manufacturer, through the wholesaler, to the retailer seems the most common, other parties can be involved in the distribution of products. Franchisors and endorsers are just two additional parties that may be involved.

Such parties will not be liability for warranty claims under the Uniform Commercial Code. They are not directly involved in the "sale of goods" and the U.C.C. will not apply. The question arises, however, as to whether they may be liable in tort.

Negligence claims are, of course, always available to an injured party. As with most negligence claims, this one will usually fail due to the difficulty of proving that the defendant failed to use reasonable care.

Strict liability in tort has not been used against such parties. Endorses are not the type of party that strict liability was intended to cover. Franchisors are usually not directly involved in the manufacturing or marketing of goods. They are usually selling a business plan for the others to engage in the manufacturing and marketing of goods.

One particular type of claim has proved successful against endorsers. Since endorsers typically make statements about the quality of goods, the possibility of a misrepresentation claim has been raised. Courts have tended to limit such claims to negligent misrepresentation. Of course, proving that the defendant failed to use reasonable care in making a false statement remains the difficult issue of proof.

H. Leases

Leases have also proven to raise difficult issues for courts when confronted with product liability claims. It would appear that a "lease" is not a "sale" and that, therefore, products liability actions should not apply. The Uniform Commercial Code assumes that it applies to "sale of goods" and should not, therefore, apply to leases. Strict liability in tort applies to sale of products and, therefore, should not apply to leases. The law, however, has not been that clear.

Parties can, of course, be sued in negligence for the lease of a dangerous product. Again, the major issue for a plaintiff in such a case is to show that the defendant had a duty and failed to use reasonable care. Proving that a failure to inspect the product was the cause of the injury is difficult

There has been some issue raised about making strict liability applicable to the leases of products. The courts have analyzed such cases in much the same way that the sale of used products was analyzed. Courts looked at the purposes of strict liability and tried to determine if those purposes would be met by applying the basis to leases.

In some commercial examples, the courts have found that the lease is so similar to an actual sale, strict liability should apply. It is easy to imagine going to a new car dealership in order to select a new car. Once the car is selected, the buyer will then decide whether to buy or lease the automobile. If the automobile is leased, the lease will run for multiple years. In those types of transactions, the courts have been unable to find any real differences between a lease and a sale. The plaintiff could bring an action for strict liability.

Using the same logic, courts have extended warranty claims to such leases. Recognizing that such a lease accomplishes the same purposes as a sale, it appeared appropriate to apply the provisions of the Uniform Commercial Code.

I. Real Estate

Real estate transactions should not have any products liability issues. Real estate law developed in its own area and has special rules that apply only to the transfer of real property. The Uniform Commercial Code applies to the sale of goods and not real estate. None of the warranties should apply to real estate transactions. Strict liability in tort for product injuries is a particular basis of liability limited to products. It should also exclude real estate transactions. Negligence law has similar problems. Since real property transfers usually require a written agreement, the only liability that can be found must be mentioned in that written agreement. Negligence should also be excluded from real property transfers.

That analysis is followed for most real property transfers. When property law was developed the sale of the land itself was the primary feature of the sale. If there were any buildings or structures on the land, there were merely considered incidental to the transfer. The world has, of course, changed. Most modern real estate transactions are primarily concerned with the building that is on the real estate. When people buy homes, they are rarely concerned with the quality of the soil. They are more concerned with the structure and the important features of that structure. People are not buying soil, they are buying a living space with hot and cold water, heating and air conditioning. This shift to the purchase of living space is creating a shift in the law.

In the post World War II housing market, a new form of home building took place. In New Jersey, a builder created a whole subdivision of similar homes. The buyers could select colors, but the basic structures of the homes were identical. This was especially true of heating, plumbing and mechanical features of the homes. When a home buyer was injured by some of the plumbing features, the courts began to look at the homes differently than traditional real property sales. The homes began to look like mass produced products. As such, some of the traditional theories of negligence law began to apply. The courts have not moved in that direction for custom built homes.

In this narrow area some possibility of applying products liability law is occurring. Where the home is more of a mass produced home, then the traditional law of negligence may be applied. The courts, however, have been unwilling to move into strict liability. The theories of warranty under the Uniform Commercial Code have also not been applied to real property sales. Some jurisdictions, however, are experimenting with similar theories and creating a new implied warranty of habitability. Such movement is a minority. For many jurisdictions, the traditional law of property applies and the home buyer is not able to seek a remedy unless it is specified in the contract of sale or deed for the property.

J. Services

The delivery of services provides a difficult area for products liability law. Like many of the topics in this chapter it initially appears to be simple. Where a prospective defendant provides the delivery of a service, then the only basis of liability ought to be negligence. Doctors, lawyers, architects, plumbers, cosmetologist, and all others in the service fields are held to a standard of care based upon their area. When errors occur and litigation arises it is based on negligence and falls under the broad heading of malpractice. The delivery of a service should not give rise to an action for breach of warranty under the Uniform Commercial Code or strict liability in tort.

There are times, however, that those delivering a service also provide a product with the service. A doctor may implant a medical device during surgery, or a cosmetologist may apply a permanent wave to hair during a beauty shop visit. Lawyers may even hand over a will after an office consultation with a client. Courts have had to review the application of strict liability to these actions that appear to be a "sales-service" hybrid.

When the courts get a case that appears to be a "sales-service" hybrid, it is necessary to look at the overall circumstances of the case to determine what the most important features of the particular transaction are. Did the consumer seek the service or did the consumer seek the product? Imagine, for example, that a consumer goes to a physician with irregular heart beat. The patient is probably seeking the expert advice and counsel of the physician. If the physician decides that it will be necessary to install a pace maker, the sale of that pace maker is not the primary factor in the transaction. The patient was seeking a service which just happened to have the delivery of a product involved. If an injury occurs, any action against the physician would be for negligence. If the pacemaker proved to be defective, there could be a strict liability action against the manufacturer, but not against the physician. Imagine, however, that while the patient was in the hospital, a visitor came to see the patient. When the visitor came into the hospital, the visitor stopped in the hospital gift shop to purchase a box of chocolates for the patient. When the patient ate a few chocolates, imagine that a toxic substance in the chocolates caused an injury. Although the sale of chocolates was in a place normally reserved for the delivery of medical services, the sale of that box of candy was a true sale. The courts would determine that the transaction looked like the sale of a product and strict liability could be used.

Similar issues have arisen with beauty shops. Where, for example, a cosmetologist applied a permanent wave, the permanent wave could cause injury. When the customer has sued, the courts have treated such transactions as the sale of a product. Although the application of the permanent wave appears to be a service, the overall transaction looks more like the sale of goods.

There are numerous cases in the area of "sales-service" hybrid. They are intended to be dealt with on a case by case basis and analyzed according to their individual circumstances. There is no clear rule of thumb, but one feature tends to appear regularly. Where the defendant is one of the traditional professions, then the case is usually treated as a service. Those traditional professions are, of course, doctors, lawyers, architects, engineers, and other such groups. Where the defendant is not one of the traditional professions, such as cosmetologist, plumbers, and the like, then the transaction is more likely to be treated as a sale of a product.

K. Contribution, Indemnity

It should be clear from the above material in this chapter that more than one defendant may be sued and held liable in a products liability action. When one or more defendants are held liable, those defendants may feel that they have a claim against other defendants. Wholesalers, for example, may feel that they should be able to recover some or all of their losses against the retailers or the manufacturers of the product. Such defendants will sue the other possible defendants for contribution or indemnity.

1. Tort or Contract

Contribution has become a part of the typical tort action. Where one defendant has been sued and is exposed to possible liability for a tort, that defendant will usually bring in other possible defendants. The first defendant will be seeking to make sure that if he or she is made to pay a judgment, other responsible parties will have to provide reimbursement for some of the loss.

Contribution usually provides that defendants who are jointly liable for a loss can be made to reimburse each other up to a pro rata share of the judgment that has been paid. Under traditional joint and several liability, the plaintiff does not have to seek the joint shares from each of the defendants. The plaintiff may sue one or all of the defendants and then take one or all of the defendants to judgment. The plaintiff can then recover that judgment from any of the defendants held liable. The defendants must pursue the right to contribution among each other.

The claim of contribution seems to be based upon the idea that the defendants are usually about equally at fault. Where there is a substantial difference in the degree of fault among the defendants, indemnity is possible. Where contribution allows a defendant to receive a pro rata share of the losses from each of the other defendants, indemnity allows the defendant to receive back all that was paid.

Indemnity allows the paying defendant to receive back from other defendants all that was paid under certain, limited circumstances. Indemnity applies where the paying defendant was held due to the operation of law and the other defendants were actually at fault.

In the products liability area, the application of indemnity may occur due to the operation of strict liability. Where a retailer or wholesaler is liable in strict liability for a full judgment due to having sold a product in a defective condition, one of those defendants may seek indemnity from the manufacturer. The claim will be that the wholesale or retailer had no knowledge of the defect and is being held liable due only to the operation of strict liability. The manufacturer, however, made the defective product and there even may be allegations of negligence on the part of the manufacturers. Under such conditions, the wholesaler or retailer may be able to recover for indemnity from the manufacturer.

Application of warranty law to the issue of contribution and indemnity raises a few important issues. The Uniform Commercial Code and the courts do not speak of this issue in the same terms as are used in tort law. In fact, however, the parties may be seeking something like indemnity.

It is possible that the parties may have entered into an express indemnity arrangement. In setting up this distribution chain, the manufacturer, wholesaler and retailer may have agreed, by contract, which would be ultimately liable for any losses due to products liability claims. If such a contract provision existed, it would be enforced. Indemnity, however, may be available without such agreement.

Under the Uniform Commercial Code there is an implied warranty of merchantability. If the manufacturer produces a defective product, that product would breach the implied warranty of merchantability. When the manufacturer sold the product to the wholesaler, the breach of that implied warranty would extend to that party. When the wholesaler sold the product to a retailer, the retailer would be the beneficiary of such a warranty from the wholesaler. If the ultimate consumer, therefore, were to sue the retailer for injuries due to a defective product, the retailer could sue the wholesaler for the breach of that implied warranty. They wholesaler could then sue the manufacturer for the breach of the same warranty. In short, each party in the chain of distribution would have a claim back up that chain against the party above them. The recovery would be in the nature of indemnity.

2. The Workers Compensation Problem

The operation of products liability law, contribution and indemnity raises a difficult problem when the injury happens in the work place. This type of accident is not uncommon. It has been estimate by some that over half of the products liability cases that have been filed are actually work place injuries. Although workers' compensation law is a matter of state law and there are differences among the 50 states, some general concepts may be understood.

When an injury happens in the work place, the employee is entitled to medical care and, when necessary, some payment for loss of wages. That loss of wages payments are based upon calculation of disability. If the employee dies from the injuries, the family is entitled to some death benefits. It is not necessary for the employee or the family of the deceased to prove fault. The payment of the medical costs and disability acts like insurance. Since the employee is entitled to these payments, those payments are the exclusive remedy for recovery against the employer. Although the disability payments may not provide a full replacement for future lost wages, the employee cannot sue the employer. The assumption behind the statute is that both parties gain some benefits and both lose some options. The employee gets the certain sure recovery of some payments while giving up the right to full recovery under tort. The employer gets reduced payouts by guaranteeing that some payments will be made.

Although the workers' compensation payments are the exclusive remedy against the employer, the employee or family members of a deceased employee may sue third parties who were also responsible for the accident. This is where the possibility of a products liability action arises.

Imagine that an employer purchases large machinery from a third party for use in a factory owned and operated by the employer. The employee works in the factory and uses one of the large machines that was purchased for such use. If the employee is injured by the machine, the employee would be entitled to workers' compensation recovery. That recovery of workers' compensation payments would be due from the employer's insurance carrier without any proof of fault.

The employee, however, might want to sue the manufacturer of the machine claiming that the machine was defective and the defect was the cause of the injury. If the employee could prove those facts, the employee could recover a substantial tort judgment using strict liability. Since the employer's original payment of workers' compensation benefits were insurance payments, the operation of insurance law would then come into effect. The original insurance carrier would be entitled to subrogation. Subrogation would allow the insurance carrier to reclaim, from the employee, any amount paid for workers' compensation. After the action is over, the workers' compensation carrier would have all of the workers' compensation payments returned, while the employee would have the money remaining from the tort judgment gained against the manufacturer.

When this type of action has occurred, the manufacturer of the machine has sued the employer for contribution or indemnity. The allegation against the employer is usually that the employer was somewhat negligent in setting up the equipment, defining appropriate work rules, or supervising the employees. If the manufacturer and the employer are held to be equally at fault, then traditional contribution law would indicate that the manufacturer ought to be able to recover back a pro rata share from the employer. If the manufacture was held liability under strict liability while the employer was negligent, then the manufacturer ought to be able to recover back the full judgment under indemnity. Courts, however, have not been inclined to allow contribution or indemnity in these types of situations.

As noted earlier, workers' compensation was set up as a balanced system to reach important public policy concerns. It was felt to be important to make sure that injured workers got certain, sure recovery when they were injured on the job. To assist employers in providing this recovery, clear, specific, and limited amounts of recovery are specified. Courts have stated that if third parties are able to bring employers back into the litigation and recover substantial judgments for contribution or indemnity, the courts would be doing indirectly what the law prohibits doing directly. The workers' compensation payments are suppose to be the "exclusive" remedy in a work place injury. The law cannot allow the third party manufacture to bring the employer back into the litigation.

The problem with this result is that it can work an injustice. If the employer was substantially at fault, then the employer may be profiting by being careless. An employer could set unrealistic quotas for employees and encourage them to bypass safety measures. Then, when an employee is injured on a large machine, the manufacturer would be liable for large judgments, and the employer would wind up getting all of the workers' compensation payments that were made back by the operation of subrogation law.

Some states have sought to reach a compromise in this area. Those states have not allowed the manufacturer to receive back full contribution or indemnity payments. They have allowed, however, the manufacturer to receive a contribution payment equal to the amount of the workers' compensation that the employer would have paid. This means that the employer does not get to keep the amount of money regained through subrogation, but must, instead, turn it over to the third party manufacturer.

Parties Checkpoints

- The proper plaintiff in a tort claim is the foreseeable plaintiff.

- The proper plaintiff in a warranty action is specified by the alternatives available under Uniform Commercial Code 2-318.

- Component part manufacturers, manufactures, wholesalers and retailers may be held liable in negligence, strict liability, and for warranties.

- Used product dealers may be held liable for negligent misrepresentation.

- Endorsers may be held liable in negligence.

- Successor corporations are not liable for claims against prior corporations except under certain specific circumstances.

- Contribution allows joint tortfeasors to recover back a pro rata share of judgments that were paid.

- Indemnity allows a paying defendant to recover back the total amount paid.

Chapter 7

Manufacture

Manufacture Roadmap
- Determine the basic problem for mis-manufactured products.
- Understand the most common methods of proof.
- Work with the common food and beverage problems.

In some ways, the mis-manufactured product is the easiest claim for the plaintiff. It is important to recognize that there are three ways that a product may be defective. It may be mis-manufactured, mis-designed, or inadequately warned about. The mis-manufactured product is one that did not come from the factory in the form that the manufactured intended it to. It is this difference from design that makes the action easier for the plaintiff to prove. In the area of mis-design, courts have created multiple test to try to define the concept of defect. When, however, the product comes from the factory with parts missing, put together incorrectly, or not working, that looks defective. Courts have been inclined to allow recovery for the plaintiff with evidence that merely pointed out those features. It is difficult for a manufacturer to defend such claims when the product that caused the injury did not look or perform as the manufacturer intended for it to. These cases, therefore, tend to be more concerned with the proof of facts rather then difficult legal issues. The problem is whether the plaintiff can prove that the specific product that caused the injury did, in fact, come off the assembly line in a condition different from expected. (For a lesson on manufacturing defects, see CALI Lessons, Liability for Defectively Manufactured Products, http://www2.cali.org)

It must be kept in mind that mis-manufacture is not a separate basis of liability. It is, instead, a set of facts or circumstances that allows the plaintiff to prove the underlying facts to bring a products liability action within one of the basis of liability. Mis-manufacture cases may rely upon negligence, strict liability, warranty, or misrepresentation if the elements of those bases can be proven.

A. Departure from Design

Departure from design is merely one way of offering proof by the plaintiff when the allegation is that the product is defective due to mis-manufacturing. The plaintiff will seek to prove that the product came off the assembly line in a form that was not intended by the manufacturer. Most products have been designed and tested with particular design features intended. When the product does not meet the manufacturer's own design requirements, plaintiffs will seek to prove that. As stated earlier in this chapter, departure from design is not a legal theory on which a plaintiff can base a case. It is, instead, a method of proving facts that will give rise to an inference that the product is in a defective condition unreasonably dangerous.

Examples of departure from design are easy to imagine. They include those products that are missing parts or have parts that were improperly installed. An automobile, that is designed to have a certain number of bolts holding on important features and is discovered to have a few of those bolts missing, appears to be a mis-manufactured product.

The difficulty with finding manufacturing flaws in the product raises additional proof issues. Frequently after a product has caused an injury, it will be found to have numerous problems. An automobile, for example, that is alleged to have been defective will have now been in a wreck. The plaintiff will point to some of the defects in the automobile and claim that those defects were in the product and caused the wreck. The defendant will point to those same defects and say they arose while the automobile was being wrecked. In short, the plaintiff will claim that the defect was the cause of the accident while the defendant will claim that the accident caused the defects.

Because of the difficulty in pointing out defects and then offering opinions as to whether those defects were the cause of the accident or caused by the accidents, these cases require expert witnesses. The experts will need to be knowledgeable engineers and designers for the types of products that are at issue. They will need to study the product and be ready to testify about the nature of the problems and whether those problems were the cause of or caused by the wreck.

B. Malfunction Doctrine

The malfunction doctrine is another way of providing evidence that will give rise to an inference that a product is defective. The basic idea is to prove that the product did not perform in the manner in which it was expected to perform. The evidence that the product malfunctioned becomes evidence that the product is defective.

The malfunction doctrine appears similar to the traditional tort doctrine of res ipsa loquitur. It is not, however, the same as res ipsa loquitur. Res ipsa loquitur is a narrow inference that only applies to negligence actions. Where res ipsa loquitur applies, it is in inference that there was a breach of the duty in negligence.

The malfunction doctrine can have an impact regardless of the basis of liability. Whether the plaintiff is suing in tort or warranty, the fact that the product malfunctioned becomes evidence that the product is defective. That defect may be used in any claim.

C. Food and Beverages

Food and beverage cases are some of the oldest forms of products liability actions. The finding of substances that were not suppose to be in food has resulted in the development of law concerning adulterated food items. With the appearance of soft drinks in returnable bottles in the 20th century, the problem with exploding bottles arose. Both of these types of actions were sufficiently common to give rise to special rules of law.

1. Exploding bottles

Exploding soft drink bottle cases were common during the period when such drinks were sold in returnable bottles. The industry would purchase large numbers of bottles and then fill them at bottling plants. When consumers purchased the bottled drinks, the consumer had to pay an additional deposit on the bottle. When the consumer returned the bottle to the retailer, the consumer got a refund on the deposit. The retailer would then return the bottles to the bottling plant for refilling. The bottles would, of course, undergo a substantial sterilization process and inspection before refilling. After refilling, the bottled soft drinks would reenter the market. Such returnable bottles could be sold and refilled numerous times. At times, they would explode.

When soft drink bottles exploded, courts determined that there were probably three possible reasons that the bottles exploded. Those reason were (1) the bottle was initially mis-manufactured and had a weak spot on the bottle; (2) the bottle was overfilled or overcharged with carbonation when it was refilled; or (3) the bottle had been chipped or damaged at some point. Any of those three reasons could cause a bottle to explode. It should be noticed when looking at the three possible reasons for bottles exploding, two of them are clearly within the control of the manufacturer. Producing a bottle that is weak from the beginning or overfilling a bottle is within the control of the manufacturer. It would be possible, however, for a bottle to be damaged or chipped by someone other than the manufacturer.

The possibility that a bottle could explode for only one of three reasons, and at least two of those reasons were in the control of the manufacturers, led the courts to favor plaintiffs with these types of cases. The existence of exploding soft drink bottles would frequently lead courts to declare that the evidence of the explosion was an inference of fault on the part of the manufacturer or bottler. In such cases, the defendant would have to prove that the plaintiff was the cause of his or her own harm.

One of the classic exploding soft drink bottle cases was *Escola v. Coca Cola Bottling Co*, 150 P.2d 436 (Cal. 1944). That case was discussed in Chapter 1. In that case, the court went so far as to note that the existence of an exploding soft drink bottle raised the doctrine of res ipsa loquitur. There was a concurring opinion to that case by Justice Traynor. He opined that the what the court should do is just admit that there was a doctrine of strict liability in such cases.

Regardless of the methods used by the courts, exploding soft drink bottle cases tended to favor the plaintiffs. Plaintiffs could usually recover the damages in an action against the manufacturer or bottler. Such cases are rare today. When soft drink companies moved away from returnable bottles and began to use cans and non-returnable bottles, the containers stopped exploding.

2. Adulterated Products

The more difficult cases for plaintiffs was and continue to be the adulterated food cases. These cases arise when a plaintiff finds something in food or drink that does not appear appropriate. Adulterated soft drink bottle cases were also common during the period of returnable bottles. With the move to non-returnable bottles, adulterated soft drink cases seem to have disappeared. There are, however, several problems that make other adulterated food cases a continuing difficulty for plaintiffs.

The first problem confronted by plaintiffs is a mere proof of facts problem. A plaintiff may consume some food or drink and subsequently become sick. An allegation by the plaintiff that the food or drink caused the illness will be difficult to substantiate. The defendants will allege that the plaintiff consumed different things throughout the day and any of those items may have caused the illness. In addition, the defendants will allege that the plaintiff just came down with a virus and the consumption of food and drink had nothing to do with the illness. Proving that the consumption of a particular item of food or drink caused a particular injury is very difficult.

There are times, however, when the proof of the connection between the consumed item and the injury is easier. Even when that fact can be proven, difficult legal issues arise.

One of the first problems encountered by plaintiffs is to prove that the foreign substance was in the product when it left the manufacturer. Courts appear to be concerned that some tampering may have occurred after the food left the manufacturer or seller. To overcome this issue, plaintiffs are required to prove a chain of custody. The plaintiff will need to show the presence of control of the product from the manufacturer to the plaintiff. This evidence will prove the absence of tampering.

Even after overcoming those initial issues, problems remain. When a plaintiff consumes food or drink and encounters something that should not be there, cases have tended to try to work through a series of legal tests to determine if liability should arise. One of the earliest tests of whether liability should attach was the "foreign-natural" rule. As originally stated, courts would indicate that if a plaintiff was injured by a natural substance in food then there would be no liability. If the substance was foreign, however, then there would be liability. Distinguishing between foreign and natural became the issue to litigate.

It would be obvious that if someone found metal parts, glass, or stones in food, that would be foreign. Such things are not natural to food and beverage. The problem, however, was not that simple.

A good example of the difficulties with the foreign natural test can be seen in *Webster v. Blue Ship Tea Room*, 198 N.E.2d 309 (Mass. 1964). In that case the plaintiff was eating fish chowder in a restaurant and encountered a bone in the soup. The difficulty should be obvious. The plaintiff alleged that bones were not natural to soup. The defendants, however, alleged that bones were natural to fish. After reviewing several recipes for fish chowder, the court determined that a good New England fish chowder had large chunks of fish in it. As such, a consumer would be led to expect the presence of bones.

As can be seen by that analysis, several things began to occur. Courts began to think in terms of what consumers expect when they consume food. One might expect fish bones in fish chowder, but one would not expect meat bones in hot dogs. This may have been some of the earliest formations of the consumer expectation test that would be a part of the Restatement (Second) of Torts § 402A comments. The consumer expectation test is discussed more fully in chapter 8. This analysis also allowed courts to review numerous cases dealing with such things as canned tuna and canned chicken. Where consumers found the existence of bones in such products, the courts were inclined to hold they were not defective. Consumers should be on notice that bones may appear in such items.

There is an interesting problem, however, with such food items. There are times when sellers will market canned meats and the packaging will say "boneless." Where that occurs, the possibility of actions for misrepresentation and express warranty arise. Although a seller may be able to avoid liability for strict liability or negligence when a bone appears in a meat product, misrepresentation and warranty claims are different. Where the manufacturer claims the product is "boneless," the presence of bone will breach the warranty or be a misrepresentation.

Manufacture Check Points

- Proving that the specific product that caused the injured differed from the intended design of the product may be sufficient to recover in products liability.

- Proving that the specific product that caused the injury malfunctioned may create an inference that the product was defective.

- Adulterated food cases are some of the earliest product liability cases and gave rise to:
  - Foreign-natural rule, and
  - Consumer Expectation test.

- Proof of adulterated food cases usually required the plaintiff to prove a chain of custody.

- Exploding bottle cases usually created an inference of defect.

Chapter 8

Design

Design Roadmap

- Determine which bases of liability are available for design defects.
- Understand the tests that have been created to determine when a design defect is in a defective condition unreasonably dangerous.
- Analyze the proof problems that arise with design defects.
- Understand the issues concerned with unavoidable unsafe products.

Design defect cases may be the most difficult to try by both plaintiffs and defendants and the most difficult for plaintiffs to win. In the design defect case, the plaintiff and defendant agree that the product looks exactly as the defendant intended for the product to look. The plaintiff is alleging, however, that the design of the product is, itself, defective. This requires the plaintiff to show that the product could have been designed in a better manner. (For a lesson on design defects, see CALI Lessons, Liability for Defectively Designed Products, http://www2.cali.org.)

The basis of liability for such cases has also created some degree of difficulty. Negligence is always a possible basis of liability. Where the product can be proven to be a design defect, the implied warranty of merchantability may also be available. The difficult issue is whether design defect cases can be true strict liability in tort cases.

After the adoption of Restatement (Second) of Torts § 402A, strict liability, there began a debate about the application of strict liability to design cases. In fact, the major tests that are used for such strict liability have been developed in the design defect cases. Those tests are discussed, in detail, below. Some noted text writers argued that strict liability should have never been used for design defect and negligence should be the available tort remedy. Courts across the country are split on this issue. Some maintain that they follow a form of strict liability for design cases and use one of the tests noted below. Some claim that strict liability and negligence are sufficiently similar as to not require a distinction. Some continue to apply negligence alone to design cases.

The adoption of Restatement (Third) of Products Liability put the weight of the American Law Institute behind those that maintain design cases should be limited to negligence. The test and analysis provided by the Restatement (Third) focuses on the reasonableness and foreseeability of the design flaws. This leaves the courts applying a negligence test. It will be necessary in the future to see where jurisdictions go on this issue.

Although there is a continuing debate about whether true strict liability should be used for design cases, there are jurisdictions that apply that basis. The following material discusses the law and rules that have developed in that area. The key to each of the following test is how the law seeks to focus the consideration. The courts have tended to say that strict liability focuses on the condition of the product and not on the conduct of the defendant. If the law were to focus on the conduct of the defendant then the basis of liability would be negligence. As each of the following tests are discussed, notice how the law allows the fact finder to focus on the condition of the product.

A. Tests to Use

1. Consumer Expectation

The first test that was considered for a product being in a defective condition unreasonably dangerous was the consumer expectation test. The test is not mentioned specifically in Restatement (Second) of Torts § 402A, but it is mentioned in the comments to that section. The test would ask the jury to decide whether the product performed as would be expected by the ordinary and reasonably prudent consumer. As the original test, it was, at one time, the majority rule.

Notice first that the test seems to be something of an outgrowth of the "foreign/natural" rule that arose in adulterated food cases. Where the foreign natural rule began to ask whether the food appeared as expected by a consumer, this rule expands beyond food. The question about performance of the product extends to any product.

It is also important to note how the rule focuses on the product and not on the conduct of the manufacturer or seller. The test asks about the expectations of the consumer and does not ask about the conduct of the manufacturer. By asking about the expectations of the consumer, the test allows the jury to study the "reasonableness" of the product and be unconcerned with the reasonableness of the behavior of the manufacturer. In short, the reasonableness or unreasonableness of the actions of the manufacturer are irrelevant to the decision. The only question is whether the product itself was reasonably fit.

It is easy to imagine the application of the consumer expectation test. When a consumer buys an ordinary kitchen butcher knife, the consumer has clear expectations about that purchase. The consumer will be expecting to use the knife to cut up meats, vegetables, and fruit for ordinary preparation in the home kitchen. While cutting up items in the kitchen, the ordinary consumer will be aware of obvious items. If the butcher knife is sharp enough to cut up meat to be used for food, it will also be sharp enough to cut the consumer's hand. If the consumer happened to injure him or herself by cutting a finger while preparing a meal in the kitchen, there would be no products liability action. The ordinary consumer would expect that the knife could cut his or her hand.

Imagine, however, that something different happens. While the consumer is busy cutting up a chicken in the kitchen, the butcher knife blade snaps in half. After snapping in half, a portion of the blade flies off the knife and sticks in the consumer's hand. The consumer would now have a products liability action. The ordinary consumer would expect that a butcher knife would be able to cut up a chicken without breaking apart.

As the law developed concerning the application of the phrase "defective condition unreasonably dangerous," courts began to have trouble with application of the consumer expectation test. The primary difficulty was that there were some products found to be so complex that ordinary consumers did not have expectations. The complexity was just beyond the ordinary expectations of consumers. Consumers might, for example, have expectations about the basic workings of an automobile, but they would not have expectation about the more complex engineering necessary to make that automobile safe. Courts found that the results reached with application of the consumer expectation test were not always appropriate. With the difficulties with the consumer expectation tests, other tests began to be suggested.

2. Risk/Utility

Text writers began to suggest that the courts should move to a risk/utility analysis to determine whether a product was in a defective condition unreasonably dangerous. The theory behind this test seems simple. Since the question is whether the product itself is "reasonable," then the courts should apply the traditional tort theory of risk/utility to the product itself. Notice again that the risk/utility analysis is to be applied to the product and not the conduct of the manufacturer. The question to be determined is whether the quality or safety of the product itself is sufficiently reasonable to be on the market.

Return for a moment to the example of the kitchen butcher knife. Again, if the butcher knife was sharp enough to cut meat, it will also cut a consumers hand. If a consumer, while cutting up chicken, happened to also cut his or her own hand, there would be no products liability action. The jury would be asked to compare the risks and the utilities of the knife. There is a risk that a butcher knife would cut someone's hand. The utility of having butcher knives, however, far outweighs that risk. Households could not continue to prepare meals in the kitchen without ordinary kitchen knives. The mere fact that someone might cut their finder is not sufficient to outweigh the utility.

Imagine again, however, that the blade on the knife snaps and injuries the consumer. The risk/utility test will also allow a products liability test to proceed. It appears possible for manufacturers to produce kitchen knives that will last a long time without breaking in half. If a manufacturer makes a knife that is prone to break, that risk is greater than the utility of having knifes.

The risk/utility analysis, or some form of that test, has become the majority rule in the United States. It appears to allow juries to seek to find whether a particular product is in a "defective condition unreasonably dangerous" without looking at the conduct of the manufacturer. The risk/utility analysis allows the detailed focus on the product.

3. Knowledgeable Manufacturer

It was suggested that the risk/utility analysis could be used but with a better way of explaining the analysis to the jury. Some text writers came up with a proposed jury instruction that could best be called the knowledgeable manufacturer test. While still relying on an underlying risk/utility analysis, the method of explaining the test to the jury was thought to be easier for the jury to understand.

When the test is explained to the jury, the jury is asked to assume that the manufacturer had knowledge of the defect or risks associated with the product and then decide whether the manufacturer acted reasonably in putting the product on the market. At first glance, this test appears merely to adopt negligence as the standard and then look to the conduct of the manufacturer. Notice, however, that the test explains to the jury that the jury is to assume that the manufacturer had notice of defects and risks. It is not necessary for the plaintiff to prove that the manufacturer had such notice. That notice will be assumed even if the manufacturer alleges that he or she did not have notice. Because of the assumption that the risks were known by hindsight, some have referred to this test as the "hindsight" test.

The value of this test is that it allows judges, lawyers and juries to use language and tests that seem to be familiar. The asking whether the manufacturer behaved reasonably is the old test for negligence. By assuming the knowledge of risk, however, the jury is actually focusing on the product. The question about the reasonable behavior of the manufacturer becomes a question about a hypothetical manufacturer. The jury is actually being asked whether a hypothetical, reasonable manufacturer would have put the product on the market knowing of the risks.

Applying this test to our example of the butcher knife, one can see that the same results would be reached. If the injury was the cutting of a finger by the consumer, there is no action. Even if the manufacturer knew that consumers could cut their fingers with knives, the knife would still be marketed. If, however, the manufacturer knew that the knife blade would snap under normal home use, a reasonable manufacturer would not put that knife on the market.

4. Combinations of Tests

Those three tests have formed the basic tests for determination of whether a product is in a defective condition unreasonably dangerous. Some courts, however, have sought to use a combination of those tests in order to apply the law. California, for example, uses a combination of the risk/utility analysis and the consumer expectation test.

In California, the courts use the consumer expectation test and the risk/utility analysis as a way to determine whether a product is defective. The application of those rules is a bit complex. The plaintiff has, as a first instance, the burden of proving that the product failed to meet the ordinary expectation of a consumer. So, in the first instance, the plaintiff has to prove a breach of the consumer expectation test. If the consumer is able to meet that burden of proof, the burden of proof shifts to the defendant and the defendant can defeat liability by proving that the utility of the product exceeds the risk.

As is obvious, therefore, California is using a combination of the consumer expectation test and the risk/utility analysis. The plaintiff has the initial burden on the consumer expectation test, and that shifts the burden to the defendant to prove the utility of the product.

B. Feasible Alternative

Due to the nature of design defect claims, there is usually a fact problem that must be proven by the plaintiff. The plaintiff in design defect cases is admitting that the product is in the form exactly as designed by the manufacturer. The plaintiff's claim is that the design itself is defective. In order for the design to be "unreasonably dangerous," there must usually be a safer design. Some jurisdictions have gone as far as to require that the plaintiff prove the existence of this safer design. The safer design is usually referred to as a "feasible alternative."

The alternative that the plaintiff must show has broad requirements. It is difficult to find one clear definition of "feasible alternative," but several factors seem to be consistently stated. The alternative offered by the plaintiff must be both technically and economically feasible.

In terms of technical feasibility, the courts require that the alternative be one that experts are willing to state does exist. It is not enough for the plaintiff to claim that there is a theoretical alternative that could be available to make the product safer. There must usually be clear evidence that the technology exist to create that alternative.

It is not sufficient for the alternative to be technically feasible alone. There must also be evidence that the alternative be one that is economically feasible. By this the courts may find that it is necessary to prove that a manufacturer could, in fact, use the alternative and still market the product competitively.

In discussing the feasible alternative, some courts have referred to the need to show that the alternative offered is practical. The term practical seems to capture both the idea of technical and economic feasibility. It implies, again, that the alternative is one that manufacturers could use in the marketplace.

As the discussion of feasible alternative suggests, this is another area that requires expert testimony. The plaintiff will need to bring substantial expert testimony to show the existence of the feasible alternative.

One type of proof that the plaintiff may find useful, is the fact that other manufacturers are using the suggested alternative. Obviously, the existence of such custom evidence is not binding on the courts or jury as to what is an appropriate design. The evidence of the customary use of the alternative by other manufacturers, however, would assist in showing that the alternative design was both technically and economically feasible. It offers the fact that other manufacturers are actually able to use the alternative and market the product.

C. State of the Art

"State of the art" evidence is similar to the issue of feasible alternative. It is another way of addressing the issue of what design is currently a reasonable design for a particular product.

State of the art evidence is usually offered by the defendants. The purpose of such evidence is to show that the design of the product at issue was manufactured according to the technology and practicality that was available at the time of that manufacturing. This evidence has been suggested as being a defense in some jurisdictions or merely an inference of no defect in others. It is, at least, a way for defendants to offer evidence that the product was not in a defect condition unreasonably dangerous at the time of manufacture.

State of the art evidence is merely what the name suggests. The defendants will offer expert testimony that the design of the product in question was manufactured according to the reasonable design features available at that time.

It should be noted that "feasible alternative" and "state of the art" are actually talking about the same issue. Feasible alternative is usually offered by the plaintiff to prove that the product could have been designed in a safer manner. State of the art is usually offered by the defendant to prove that the product was reasonably safe at the time it was designed.

D. Dangerous with No Feasible Alternative

In looking at design defect cases, it is obvious that many cases revolve around evidence of whether there is a feasible alternative to making the product safe. As noted above, some jurisdictions have stated that proof of a feasible alternative is a necessary element to proving the design defect. That issue, however, raises a difficult problem. There are products that are dangerous, the product has limited utility, and yet there is no feasible alternative. In such cases, there is something of an inconsistency. Appling a risk/utility analysis, the product should be held to be unreasonably dangerous. If the risk is high and the utility is low, then the product meets the test. If, however, the court requires proof of a feasible alternative, then there would be no claim if the product could not be made safer. These cases are few, but have caused the courts to split on how to handle them.

Some jurisdictions do require proof of the feasible alternative. In the absence of such proof, the product is not unreasonably dangerous. The plaintiff would not be able to recover under strict liability.

There may be a claim remaining in negligence for such products. The plaintiff may allege that after numerous accidents involving the product, the defendant is on notice of the dangers concerning that product. Continuing to market such a product would appear to be negligent.

Some jurisdictions do not require the proof of feasible alternative. Such jurisdictions would not have problems with the absence of such proof. If the risks of the product were found to exceed the utility, an action would lie.

The reality of such claims is that the actions do not arise very often. With most products, the plaintiff is able to find an expert to testify to a feasible alternative. For the few that still remain without feasible alternatives for dangerous products, they tend to leave the market place due to market forces. After a substantial number of law suits have been filed against the defendant, the defendant may decide to pull the product from the market.

E. Comment K and Pharmaceuticals

An interesting problem that arises with products without feasible alternatives is the useful product. The above discussion assumed that there was no feasible alternative and the risk of the product outweighed the utility. Imagine, however, that the product has no feasible alternative and yet the utility substantially outweighs the risks. Comments to the Restatement (Second) of Torts § 402A addressed that issue.

Comment K to Restatement (Second) of Torts § 402A spoke of the "unavoidably unsafe" product. That is the product that cannot be made safer and yet the utility substantially outweighs the risk. The primary class of products that meet this category are pharmaceutical drugs.

Pharmaceutical drugs are usually marketed after having been proven to have high utility. Those drugs may relieve suffering and save lives. The problem with most of those drugs is that they also may have serious side effects. The side effects of the drugs may be that they cause serious personal injury or death. The difficulty with the drugs is that the usually cannot be made safer. Once the chemical formula for the drug is determined, there is no way to add or take away a portion of that chemical compound and still have the drug be effective. The drug is dangerous, and yet the utility is high. It is, of course, possible to raise or lower the dosage, but even that may have an impact on effectiveness.

With products such as the drugs, the courts have determined that they are unavoidable unsafe. Although they are dangerous and there is no way to make them safer, they will not be held to be in a defective condition unreasonably dangerous.

The courts do, however, expect manufacturers to have some burden with the unavoidably unsafe products. The courts mention that the manufacturers of such items must warn users of the risks that are known. Again, pharmaceutical drugs are a good example of this process. Such drugs are developed and sold after a long testing process. During that process, it is determined whether the drug is safe and effective and the extent of side effects. When the drug is put on the market, it is necessary for the manufacturer to provide warnings that indicate the nature of the risks and side effects.

The discussion of the unavoidable unsafe product has used pharmaceutical drugs as the obvious example. The question, of course, is whether there are other examples. The comment to the Restatement (Second) of Torts § 402A did not limit the operation of that comment to drugs. The courts, however, have not found many additional examples.

Design Checkpoints

- Design defect cases may be based on negligence, strict liability in tort, or warranty.

- The basic tests that have been used to determine whether a design is in a defective condition unreasonably dangerous are:
  - Consumer expectation test;
  - Risk/utility analysis;
  - Knowledgeable manufacturer (hindsight;
  - Some combination of the above.

- Proof of a feasible alternative to the design that is being used by the defendant is helpful to the plaintiff in many jurisdictions and required proof by the plaintiff in some jurisdictions.

- Defendants may offer proof that the design was according to the state of the art at the time of manufacturing.

- Some products may have a utility that is so high that, although there are risks with the product, the product will be considered unavoidable unsafe.

Chapter 9

Warning

A. Instructions and Warnings

The failure to offer a sufficient warning may be enough to lead to liability for a defendant when a user or consumer is injured. As noted in Chapter 8, there are specific types of cases that require substantial warnings. Chapter 8 spoke of products that are of a high utility, but also have substantial risk. Those products are assumed to be unavoidably unsafe. Although the defendant will not be liable for the design of the product, the defendant has a duty to warn about known risks associated with that product. The absence of such a warning will lead to liability.

The unavoidably unsafe product is not the only product that must carry a warning. Products that carry risks must contain warnings of those risks. The extent of the duty to warn will be discussed below in section C, but the need to warn is great. In fact, the pressure felt by manufacturers to warn has led some to be concerned that the public is facing a sort of warning numbness. Most products today carry so many instructions and warnings that there is a fear that many consumers just ignore the warnings. That approach would, obviously, be counter to the reason for putting warnings on the products.

It is important to note that not all writing on a product label is a warning. Labels may have the name and product logo, instructions for proper use and then some warnings. The courts are usually most concerned with the warnings. In analyzing whether a warning was adequate, it is possible to break down the issue into about four separate elements. The courts will require that the warning be:

1. conspicuous; and
2. inform the user of the risks; and
3. inform or alert the user to the magnitude of the risk; and
4. inform the user how to safely encounter the risk.

Those elements will be discussed below.

B. Elements

1. Conspicuous

Courts will first look to see if any warning was conspicuous. There is no good definition for conspicuous, but there are facts and circumstances that may be reviewed. Usually the courts will be looking to see if the warning was such to call attention to itself so that the user would notice it.

The typical things that would alert a user can be seen. Courts will look to the location of the warning on the packaging. The courts may look at the size of the font of the warning and the color of the ink of the font. In addition, the courts will look to see if the warning is introduced by words like "WARNING" or "DANGER." Those factors will help the court determine if the warning was conspicuous.

Imagine a few examples to try to determine if a warning is conspicuous. If the warning is on the back of the package, in small print and in the same color of type as all of the other writing on the package, it is unlikely that the user will see it. That is probably not conspicuous. If, however, the warning is located on the front of the package, in large print, and in red ink where the other writing on the package is in black, then the warning looks conspicuous. The issue is whether the warning drew attention to itself.

2. Inform the User of Risks

The warning needs to inform the users of the risk associated with using the product. Merely suggesting safe use will not be sufficient if there is a possibility that the user will not understand why the safe use is necessary. Imagine, for example, that language on a bottle of cleaning fluid suggests that the cleaning fluid be added to water before being used. The user may believe that information is just a good way to save money. If, however, the real reason that the suggestion for dilution with water is made is to let the user know that the cleaning fluid is so strong that it will burn the user's hands, then that information needs to be given.

The problem noted above may be frequently discussed as the difference between instructions and warnings. Where the language appears to be merely suggesting efficient use of the product, it looks like instructions. Where it fully informs the user of the risks of using the product, it looks like a warning. The warning will not be adequate unless it informs the user of the risks.

3. Inform of the Magnitude of the Risk

When the warning informs the user of the risks associated with the product, it needs to do more than merely identify that there are risks. It needs to alert the users to the magnitude of the risks. If a product may cause serious personal injury or death, then the warning needs to say that. A user will not understand the seriousness of the risk unless the warning fully provides that information.

4. Explain How to Safely Encounter

Finally, the warning needs to inform the user how to safely encounter the risks associated with the product. It would not be useful to tell the user that there are substantial risks and then fail to inform the user on how to encounter them. The user needs to be able to deal with the product in a safe manner. The information on how to use the product safely is necessary.

C. Negligence or Strict Liability

The above material points out how the defendant may avoid liability by providing an adequate warning. That material also suggested that there was a strong duty to warn. One of the issues with warnings, however, is whether that duty is in negligence or strict liability.

It is clear that failure to warn cases can be based on negligence. The duty of the manufacturer would be to provide adequate warnings about foreseeable risk to foreseeable plaintiffs. That explanation of the duty is clearly one of negligence. By only requiring a duty to warn based on foreseeable risks, makes it a negligence duty.

The question arises, however, as to whether a manufacturer could be held liable in strict liability in tort for failure to warn. In strict liability, the manufacturer would be assumed to have known of all the risks and then required to provide warnings of those risks. If the manufacturer could be held liable for a strict liability failure to warn, then there would be no necessity of proving the foreseeability of the risk. The manufacturer would have a duty to warn of all risk both those foreseen and not foreseeable.

Although there were a few early cases that used true strict liability for failure to warn, those cases have not carried the majority rule. Most jurisdictions, even those that speak of strict liability for failure to warn, are using a form of negligence. The duty to warn of the risks arises when the risk is foreseeable. The manufacturer does not have to warn of unforeseeable risk.

The measure of foreseeability of the manufacturer, however, is high. Most courts will hold the manufacturer to have foreseen those risks that an expert or professional in the field would have foreseen. As such, the duty for failure to warn appears to be negligence. The level of negligence is that of an expert.

D. Plaintiff Would Have Acted Differently with Product

1. Issue of Causation

As with all personal injury or property damage actions, causation is an issue. The plaintiff in a products liability case must prove that the defect caused the injury. Those issues are discussed more fully in Chapter 10. Warnings, however, create special problems in causation. The typical causation problem with a failure to warn case is that the plaintiff must be able to show that he or she would have read the warning and that the warning would have caused a change in behavior.

Those two issues are frequently hard for plaintiffs to prove. Proving first that the plaintiff would have read any additional warnings is always a first step. The plaintiff may offer proof that he or she always reads warnings or there is evidence that the plaintiff actually followed some of the other instructions on the label. Absent that type of evidence, the defendants will claim the plaintiffs would not have read warnings that would have been given.

If the plaintiff can offer proof that the warning would have been read, then the plaintiff must still prove that the existence of a better warning would have caused that plaintiff to change behavior. The plaintiff must be able to offer proof that he or she would have followed the warning.

2. Read and Heed Presumption

The proof problems with causation and warnings have led the courts to create a presumption. Referred to as the "read and heed" presumption, the courts provide some assistance to plaintiffs. The presumption is that if the defendant had placed a warning on the label, it would have been read and heeded by the plaintiff. This presumption, therefore, assists the plaintiff in proving the two parts of the difficult causation issue that arises in most warning cases.

E. Who Must Be Warned?

There is a broad question of who must be warned in the failure to warn cases. It is obvious that in ordinary cases, the user or consumer must be warned. For most consumer products, this is easy to visualize. A consumer purchases a product and the warning will accompany the product. If the consumer purchases a toaster, there will usually be a little booklet that comes with the appliance. The booklet will have several pages of instructions and a list of warnings. Such a delivery of warnings should be adequate.

Some products are not made in a way that providing booklets is the best way to deliver the warnings. When a consumer purchases a simple hand tool, proving a full booklet may not be appropriate. Imagine, for example, that a consumer purchases a hammer. It is unlikely that the consumer would read any booklet provided with the hammer. For such warnings as not striking certain types of objects or suggesting the use of goggles, stickers with the warning can be placed directly on the tool. For an easy example, notice a car tire. The size of the tire and the appropriate amount of air pressure are usually stated on the side of the tire.

In short, for most products, the manufacturer needs to deliver the warning to the user or consumer along with the product. The exact method of delivery of the warning will depend on the facts and circumstances of the product. Not all products can carry the warning directly to the user or consumer. Some products create special problems.

1. Bulk Supplier

Some products may be delivered in such a way that warnings cannot be attached to the product and delivered to the user. Imagine, for example, that a supplier of sand or grit is delivering train cars full of the product to a factory. The factory will then unload the sand or grit to use in a process in that factory. The individual employees of the factory need to be warned to use some type of mask to keep from inhaling the sand or grit.

Warning the individual employees of risks of the sand or grit is almost impossible. The warnings, for example, cannot be stamped on the side of the individual grains of sand or grit. Even raising that issue illustrates how absurd it is. The seller of the sand or grit also cannot just place the warning on the side of the railroad cars. The railroad cars will be emptied and the sand or grit carried inside the factory before the employees see it. Finally, the seller will not be able to hold individual training sessions with the employees that actually confront the risk. The seller has no right to enter the factory.

In such cases, courts have held that the seller of such bulk items can meet the duty to warn by proving adequate warnings to the immediately buyer. In the above example, the seller needs to provide adequate warnings to the factory management that is actually purchasing the sand or grit. It is the duty of the factory management to pass on those warnings.

2. Sophisticated User

A similar type of case can arise when the user of the product already knows of the risks associated with the product. As with most warning issues, the only requirement is that the user knows of the risk. If the user already knows of the risks, there is no further duty to warn. Where, therefore, the court can find that the user is a "sophisticated user," the seller of the product has no further duty to warn.

Some cases seem to find the presence of bulk sellers and sophisticated users in the same case. In the example of the bulk purchase of the sand or grit, it would be likely that the seller would also claim that the factory management is a sophisticated user. Such management probably has substantial information about the risks associate with the processes that are going on in the plant. As such, the seller would claim both "bulk sale" and "sophisticated user."

3. Learned Intermediary Rule

A special application of the "sophisticated user" rule arises in the "learned intermediary" rule. When a patient is sick and goes to a physician, that patient does not select the appropriate drug for his or her disease. The physician selects the appropriate drug and gives the patient a prescription for that drug. The patient then goes to a pharmacy to purchase the drug. As noted in earlier material, there is likelihood that the drug has a high risk of side effects associated with it. It was also noted in that earlier material that the manufacturer of that drug had a duty to warn of those risks. The question, of course, is who the manufacturer of that drug must warn.

Under the learned intermediary rule, the drug manufacturer will meet its duty to warn by providing the warning to the prescribing physician. It is assumed that the physician will use professional care in diagnosing the illness and selecting the drug. If the drug causes a severe side effect to the patient, the patient's action would be one for negligence against the physician. The patient would not have a claim for failure to warn against the drug company.

This process is so well recognized that there are techniques to make sure that physicians receive the appropriate warnings. Physicians receive letters and mailing from drug companies as well as visits from agents of the companies. All of the reports and warnings are collected annually in a book called the Physicians Desk Reference. (That book is frequently referred to as the PDR.) As long as the drug company provides the adequate warning to the physician, that company has met its duty to warn the patient.

The courts have recognized that there are some narrow sets of circumstances that may lead to a duty of the drug company to provide a warning directly to the patient. Those exceptions should be noted.

The first, and obvious, exception is the duty to warn for over the counter drugs. Over the counter drugs are marketed and distributed in a manner totally different from prescription drugs. Over the counter drugs are readily available, without prescription, in many stores. Patients can go into a store, pick the drug off the shelf and purchase it without further consultation with a physician. For those drugs, drug companies must provide the warning directly to the patient. Patients will usually find the warnings directly on the box, the bottle, or on a leaflet provided with the drug.

Another type of case that has given rise to the duty to warn the patient directly is under the circumstances of direct, mass inoculations. There have been times in the past where it has been felt necessary to provide mass inoculations of citizens for general public health. Going back many years, the public has been offered inoculations for diphtheria, polio and swine flu. When these mass inoculations occur, there is no opportunity for individual consultation by the patient with a physician. In those cases, the courts have felt there needed to be direct warning to the patient.

Another type of exception has arisen in more recent cases. In the use of birth control pills, the patient has a wide assortment of options available to prevent conception. The patient needs to select from among those options. Once the birth control pill is selected, the patient may receive a prescription that can be refilled, without consultation with a physician for 6 months to one year. Courts have determined that the patient needs to be warned directly about the risks associated with the birth control pills. With the direct involvement in the patient in selecting the drug and the long term treatment without physician guidance, the information needs to be provided to the patient. This has led, of course, to a substantial booklet being provided by the manufacturers of birth control pills.

One final exception needs to be noted. Where the drug manufacturer engages in a program of mass marketing of a drug to the public, it has been suggested that the manufacturer should also provide the warnings directly to the patient. Those opposed to this duty to warn, note that although the patient may receive the advertisement directly, the patient must still consult a physician in order to get a prescription for those drugs. Currently only one jurisdiction has required the duty to warn the patient directly when the drug has been the subject of a mass marketing campaign. That area may be one for close observation in the future to determine whether other jurisdictions will follow.

Warning Checkpoints

- In order for a warning to be adequate, it must be:

  - Conspicuous; and
  - Inform the user of the risks; and
  - Inform or alert the user to the magnitude of the risk; and
  - Inform the user how to safely encounter the risk.

- The duty to warn is based on negligence.

- The seller must warn the user or consumer.

- There are special circumstances that allow the seller to warn someone other than the user or consumer. Those special circumstances include:

  - The bulk seller, or
  - The sophisticated user; or
  - The learned intermediary.

Chapter 10

Causation

Causation Roadmap

- Understand the basic issues with cause in fact.
- Distinguish cause in fact from proximate cause.
- Analyze the basic issues with proximate cause.
- Review the special problems with causation and warning cases.

Causation is, of course, a major issue in tort law. Many of those issues have carried over to the cases that arise as products liability cases. The law is not different than the rules covered in the basic torts class. There are, however, some special application problems that arise due to the particular nature of products cases.

A. Cause in Fact

Cause in fact has several issues that must be addressed in a products liability case. Those problems can be divided into three different categories. They include, identifying the defendant, the single cause issue and the multiple cause issue. Each of those must be dealt with separately. (For a lesson on cause in fact, see CALI Lessons, Cause in Fact, http://www2.cali.org)

In products liability cases, identifying the defendant can be a difficult task. The product that caused the injury may have been destroyed by the accident itself or the plaintiffs may have discarded it before they realized that there may be a need to keep it. If the plaintiff cannot offer evidence of the proper defendant, then the defendants will win by directed verdict.

When the defendant is identified, but there is still a question of whether the product caused the injury, the easiest test to apply is the "but-for" test. This test, sometimes referred to by the Latin name of sine qua non, means that the injury would not have occurred but for the product at issue. The difficulty with the cause in fact issue is that it is not enough to show that the product brought about the injury. There must be proof that the defect in the product caused the injury. Products may fail for numerous reasons. They may be defective, but there may be other issues. The product may wear out, may have been the wrong product for the use, or may have been misused in some way. Imagine, for example, that a user selects a product that is too weak to do the job the user intends to accomplish. During use, the product fails. The cause of the injury is not a defect in the product, but misuse of the product.

Multiple possible defendants create the most difficult issues for product liability cases. Those may occur in a variety of examples. Where multiple defendants create toxic substances that harm numerous people, there is a great difficulty in showing which of the substances caused the injuries. In addition, where multiple defendants made identical products, it may be hard to prove which of the defendants made the specific product that caused the injury.

For multiple possible causes, the Restatement (Second) of Torts introduced the concept of "substantial factor." The theory was that where more than one possible cause brought about the injury, there would be liability for those causes that were a "substantial factor" in that injury. This test could be used where, for example, a plaintiff was exposed to some toxic substance. That substance may have been manufactured by multiple defendants. In addition, the plaintiff may have had some personal risks associated with contracting the disease that the substance allegedly caused. The courts would try to determine whether the named defendant was a substantial factor in bringing about the injury.

This substantial factor test has not worked as well as hoped. The Restatement (Third) of Torts is seeking to return to a form of the "but-for" test in all cause in fact examples. Future cases will have to decide what direction jurisdictions will take. (For a lesson dealing with proving cause in fact, see CALI Lessons, Proof of Cause in Fact, http://www2.cali.org)

The problem with multiple possible defendants has created a few special cause in fact tests. None of the special tests have proved particularly helpful in solving the broader problems of product liability causes. Each, however, seems to be raised a sufficient number of times to require some understanding.

An early case of *Summers v. Tice*, 199 P.2d 1 (Cal. 1948), created the doctrine of alternative liability. There, two defendants were each at fault but only one could have caused the injury. There was no clear evidence which of the defendants could have caused the injury. The court created a doctrine that could allow the plaintiff to shift the burden of causation to the defendants where there are a small number of defendants, all of whom breached a duty but only one of which could have caused the injury. Notice that *Summers v. Tice* is not a form of res ipsa loquitur. Res ipsa loquitur is an inference of breach. *Summers v. Tice* is designed to help prove causation.

Enterprise liability was created in a case called *Hall v. E.I. Du Pont De Nemours & Co.*, 345 F. Supp. 353 (E.D. N.Y. 1972). In that case, a small group of manufacturers made blasting caps. When the blasting caps failed, they destroyed themselves. It was impossible to tell who had made the particular blasting cap that caused the injury. The court created a doctrine that allowed the plaintiff to shift the burden of proving who created the product where there was a small number of defendants, they were all in court, and each participated in an agreement to make a similar product.

In *Sindell v. Abbott Laboratories*, 607 P.2d 924 (Cal. 1980), the court created a doctrine known as market share liability. In that case, a large number of manufacturers made a similar drug. That product was determined to cause cancer in the off spring of the women who took it. The injuries, therefore, would not show up for some long period after the women had taken the drugs. The court determined that where there were a large number of manufacturers, not all of whom could be in court, and who all made the same drug, each would be liable for the percentage of the judgment that the manufacturer enjoyed as a part of the original market of the drug. The plaintiff would be allowed to use this doctrine so long as the plaintiff was able to bring a sufficient number of defendants into the case so as to represent a substantial portion of the original market.

Although these doctrines would appear to be substantial benefit to the plaintiff, they are not used that often. Not all of them have been adopted by all jurisdictions. Market share liability, for example, is a substantial minority position. The other doctrines have elements that tend to narrow their use in particular cases. As such, plaintiffs retain a substantial burden in proving cause in fact in products cases.

B. Proximate Cause

Proximate cause is one of the more difficult issues in tort law. When the issue arises in a products liability case, the complexity increases. The reason for the complexity is that a products liability case may be brought in negligence or strict liability. The basic test for proximate cause is foreseeability. The problem, of course, is what must be foreseen in order for the defendant to be liable. There are a range of questions that may be raised on the topic of foreseeability.

The first circumstance that may be raised is whether the defect in the product must be foreseeable. The answer to that question may depend on whether the action is in negligence or strict liability. Where the claim is brought for strict liability, foreseeability of the defect is not an issue. Strict liability should apply whether or not the defendant could foresee the defect. In negligence, of course, the question is whether a reasonable person could have foreseen the defect. If a reasonable person could have foreseen the defect, proving that the defendant did not remedy the defect is a method of proving negligence.

A second issue is whether the use of the product was foreseeable. Although this issue is frequently raised as an issue in defense, it may also be a causation issue. Defendants would like to claim that there is no liability for misuse of the product. The courts, however, have not treated the question so simply. The issue is not whether there was misuse; the issue is whether the use of the product could have been foreseen.

A good example of foreseeable misuse occurs with an automobile accident. Many injuries during automobile accidents occur during what can be called the second impact. The first impact is when the initial accident occurs. The second impact is when something about the internal design of the automobile fails during the accident and causes the injuries. Defendants have claimed that the automobile accident is a misuse of the product and the second impact should not lead to liability. Courts have determined that automobile accidents are foreseeable misuses of that product and automobiles must be designed in light of that use. This theory is referred to as "crashworthiness."

A third issue that can be raised is whether the risk of harm must be foreseeable. In traditional negligence law, this is one of the classic tests for liability. In the famous quote by Justice Cardozo, he said that the risk reasonably to be perceived defines the duty to be obeyed. When the products liability action is brought in negligence, the plaintiff would have to prove the foreseeability of the risk of harm in order to recover.

When the products liability action is brought in strict liability, a more difficult question is raised over the foreseeability of the risk of harm. In some ways, this issue is similar to the foreseeability of the defect. Recall, for example, the knowledgeable manufacturers test for strict liability for design defects. Under that theory, the manufacturer is assumed to know of the risk of harm from the product and then the jury is asked whether a reasonable manufacturing, having such knowledge, would have put the product on the market. Under that test, there should be no need for the plaintiff to prove foreseeability of the risk of harm. In addition, under the pure risk/utility test or the consumer expectation test, the clear focus of the law is on the condition of the product. Foreseeability of the risk of harm is not an issue. In warning cases and design cases under the Restatement (Third) of Products Liability, foreseeability of the risk of harm is made an issue. It appears that this requirement of the plaintiff proving the foreseeability of the risk of harm is the feature that makes warning cases and design cases under the Restatement (Third) negligence cases.

A fourth issue that may raise questions of foreseeability is the injury received. Courts have found that the plaintiff, in difficult cases, may be required to prove there was foreseeability of the injury received. The classic example involves a person who became ill while eating in a restaurant. The person who was ill ran to the rest room, but vomited on the floor before getting to the rest room. The ill person's friend ran to the rest room to assist, only to slip and fall in the vomit on the way. The person, who fell, sued for the injury claiming the food that the friend ate was defective. *Crankshaw v. Piedmont Driving Club, Inc.*, 115 Ga. App. 820, 156 S.E.2d 208 (1967). The court held that the injury was not foreseeable.

There are several types of injuries that have raised specific problems with the proximate cause issue. Emotional distress, for example, without some additional touching or impact from the product is probably not recoverable. Where a plaintiff receives a severe physical injury from a product, the addition of pain and suffering damage is common. Where the plaintiff encounters something like foul food, bugs or vermin in food, or some other foul product, the additional of emotional distress damages may also be allowed. Where, however, the plaintiff merely observes a defective product and seeks emotional harm as a bystander injury, the courts are less likely to allow recover. The basis of that denial will be that the injury is unforeseeable.

Suicide cases raise similar issues with the issue of foreseeability. Many courts would find that suicides are unforeseeable and not allow recovery. There may be some distinctions based upon the nature of the case. Where, for example, the deceased was injured by a product and ultimately committed suicide due to the depression caused by the severe injury, a few jurisdictions would consider the claim. Where, however, the claim was merely that the deceased used the product to commit suicide; the courts would not allow recovery.

Additional problems arise in the traditional proximate cause issues of intervening and supervening causes. The traditional rules may be found to apply in most cases. Where the intervening cause was a foreseeable event, the defendant may still be liable. Where the intervening cause was not foreseeable, thus making it a supervening cause, the defendant may escape liability. Some specific products liability problems should be noted. (For a lesson covering intervening causes, see CALI Lessons, Intervening Causes, http://www2.cali.org)

One typical products liability issue arises with injuries caused by side effects from prescription drugs. As discussed in the chapter on warnings, there is an assumption that the prescribing physician will act as a learned intermediary between the manufacturer of the drug and the patient. If the injury is merely due to the patient suffering from a side effect from the drug, there will be no liability on the part of the manufacturer. If, however, the injury was the result of some defect in the drug such as foreign substances found in it, then the manufacturer could be liable.

Parental responsibility over children has led to a range of decisions in the products liability area. Common injuries that occur are the result of a child being hurt by a product when careful parental supervision could have prevented the injury. Courts have not been consistent in rulings in such cases. Although some courts see the parental negligence as a supervening cause to defeat the defendant's liability, others do not. Some would find that the purpose of strict liability requires the foreseeability of the parental negligence. In some ways, those decisions seem to equate the parental negligence to foreseeable misuse of the product. Manufacturers have sought to avoid such liability by adding substantial warnings to products that may be used in the vicinity of children.

Work place injuries also raise questions of intervening causes. When an injury occurs in the workplace, the employee will recover workers' compensation payments from the employer, but may then seek further recovery from a manufacturer of equipment that caused the injury. Frequently, the manufacturer will claim that the employer or employee removed safety equipment or avoided simple safety rules. The question becomes one of foreseeability. If the manufacturer could have foreseen these actions, then liability still attaches. If the behavior of the employer or employee was so outrageous as to not be foreseeable, then the manufacturer would escape liability. Courts have been inclined to find that such employer and employee behavior is foreseeable.

C. Special Problems with Warnings

In the chapter on warnings, a special proximate cause issue was noted. In order for the plaintiff to recover in such a case, the plaintiff must be able to prove that the presence of an adequate warning would have changed the plaintiff's conduct. This is, in fact, a causation issue. The plaintiff is proving, indirectly, that the absence of the warning was the cause of the injury. In order to prove this element, the plaintiff must usually show that he or she would have read and followed the warning.

1. Would Have Read?

Proving that the plaintiff would have read and followed the warning is typically a question of fact. Attorneys will seek to find evidence that will convince the jury that the plaintiff would have read the labels. Evidence, for example, that the plaintiff did read and follow directions that were available would be excellent proof that the plaintiff would have also followed other directions had they been included. Evidence that the plaintiff can recall details about the directions, labels and instructions are also excellent bits of evidence. Defendants will seek to show that the plaintiff did not read and would not have read any instructions. Evidence of ignoring instructions that were available would, of course, be evidence for the defendant.

2. Read and Heed Presumption

Obviously, the evidence of whether or not the plaintiff would have read and followed the warnings had they been given is speculative. Courts have created a presumption to assist the plaintiff in proof of this fact. What may be referred to as the "read and heed" presumption helps the plaintiff. This presumption allows the jury to find that had an adequate warning been provided the plaintiff would have read it and followed it.

Causation Checkpoints

- The traditional test for cause in fact is the "but for" or "sine qua non" test.
- For multiple possible causes, the substantial factor test is used.
- Foreseeability is the key term in proximate cause.
  - Foreseeability of defect should not be required for a strict liability case.
  - Foreseeability of risk should not be required for a strict liability case.
  - Foreseeability of injury is a required element of products liability cases.
  - Foreseeability of the intervening cause is an element in a products liability case.
- Warning cases require that the plaintiff offer proof that an adequate warning would have been read and followed.
- The "read and heed" presumption will assist the plaintiff in proving the causation issue in warning cases.

Chapter 11

Additional Proof Problems

Proof Roadmap

- Analyze the rules that apply to expert witnesses.
- Understand the special problems that arise in products liability cases with evidence of:
  - Custom,
  - State of the art and feasible alternatives,
  - Statutes and regulations,
  - Subsequent remedial measures.

Products liability cases raise a few special proof problems that require special attention. Although many of these issues may arise in other types of cases, they appear to have particular importance in products liability. This chapter will address some of those special problems.

A. Experts

It was noted in many of the preceding chapters that expert witnesses were necessary to prove many of the elements of the cases. Both plaintiffs and defendants find it necessary to employ and use expert witnesses though out the trials. The major issue concerning the use of expert testimony is whether the underlying science that the expert is using is valid. The Federal Rules of Evidence, Rule 702, is the rule that has been interpreted to deal with that issue.

Prior to 1993, a majority of courts felt that the test to determine whether the science was valid was a simple test. The court would ask whether the science was generally accepted in the scientific community. This test, known as the Frye test, was initially explained in *Frye v. United States*, 293 F. 1013 (D.C. Cir. 1923). In 1993, however, the United States Supreme Court made a major change in the law with *Daubert v. Merrell Dow Pharmaceuticals*, 509 U.S. 579 (1993). The *Daubert* case was, in fact, a products liability case. Plaintiffs alleged that a drug designed to reduce or limit morning sickness in pregnant women also caused birth defects in the children. The defendants, of course, denied that claim.

The opinion of the Supreme Court in *Daubert* noted that the federal rules of evidence had been adopted in 1975 which was some 50 years after the decision in Frye. The opinion further noted that the Frye decision was not cited anywhere in the federal rules or the Advisory Committee notes. Using this logic, the Court decided that the federal rules of evidence had overruled the Frye decision and that the federal rules must be interpreted to determine when science would be held valid. The Court used Fed. R. Evid. 702 to find language that could be used to justify when science was valid. (Fed. R. Evid. 702 received minor amendments in 2000 to ensure that the language of that rule was consistent with the opinions of the Supreme Court.)

The *Daubert* decision abandoned the Frye test as a strict rule to use to determine the validity of scientific evidence. In its place, the Court adopted a series of flexible factors. The trial judge would act as a "gatekeeper" to keep invalid science out of the case. The judge would apply the factors to determine what was valid.

The factors that the Court noted in *Daubert* were:

1. Whether the theory can be or has been tested;
2. Whether the theory has been subject to peer review;
3. Whether there is a known rate of error when the theory has been applied:
4. Whether there are standards and controls over the theory;
5. Whether the theory is generally accepted in the scientific community.

After the decision in *Daubert*, there remained several questions. The Supreme Court returned to the issues in the opinion in *Kumho Tire Co. v. Carmichael*, 119 S. Ct. 1167 (1999). The *Kumho Tire* case was another products liability case. This case dealt with automobile tires. The court in that opinion added further explanation. First, the question arose as to whether the *Daubert* decision only applied to scientific evidence or did it also apply to technical and other specialized knowledge areas. The Court held that the basic concepts in *Daubert* applied to all of those. It would apply when the expert was being asked to state opinions based on scientific, technical or other specialized knowledge. The Court was also faced with deciding whether the factors specified in *Daubert* were the only factors or, in fact, where they each mandatory factors. The Court held that the factors stated in *Daubert* were flexible. The trial court could use those factors, some of those factors, or other factors. Flexibility in approach was the key. The trial judge was to be the gatekeeper for the introduction of evidence and would not be bound by any one set of specified factors.

Over the 10 year period following *Daubert* and the addition of *Kumho Tire*, the lower courts had to work with the new principles. The opinions by the United States Supreme Court were so broad as to make it difficult for the trial judges to feel comfortable with making rulings. During that 10 year period some underlying principles seem to emerge.

The basic underlying principles seem to be consistently followed. The trial judge acts as gatekeeper to determine the validity of scientific evidence being presented. The judge should use the basic factors stated in *Daubert* but is not bound by them. The judge may use some, all, or even other factors to make the determination on admissibility.

B. Custom

In a basic class on tort law, evidence of customary practice is usually discussed in light of actions in negligence. The rules discussed in that context have application in products liability actions.

When the plaintiff seeks to prove negligence on the part of the manufacturers or sellers in a products case, the evidence of custom by other similar groups is admissible. Usually the plaintiff is seeking to offer such evidence in order to show that the defendant was not following customary practices. Defendants may, at times, also seek to offer such evidence. When it is being offered by the defendant, that party is usually seeking to show that he or she did, in fact, follow the customary practices of others. Although evidence of the custom is admissible, it is not conclusive on the case. The jury may consider such evidence in order to determine what reasonable parties should have done.

In strict liability cases, evidence of custom is also admissible. It is not, however, evidence of customary practices of parties. Usually in a strict liability case the plaintiffs or defendants are offering evidence of customary design. The evidence is admissible because it tends to show whether the product was at the state of the art at the time of manufacture or whether there was a feasible alternative available. Plaintiffs would be offering evidence of the customary designs by other manufacturers to show that a feasible alternative was available. Defendants would be offering such evidence in the hopes of proving that their design was according to the state of the art at the time of manufacture. As with negligence actions, the evidence of custom is not conclusive on those points. It is merely evidence that the jury can use in seeking to reach a decision on the issue of design.

C. State of the Art and Feasible Alternative

Throughout the discussion of design defects, an underlying fact was identified as important. In such cases, the plaintiff and defendant agree that the specific product that caused the injury was manufactured according to the intended design. The allegation by the plaintiff is that the design itself is defective. Courts have recognized that this allegation leaves open an important question. If the design itself is defective, then there must be a better design. Since manufacturers are not insurers of the safety of the public but are only liable when the product is unreasonably dangerous, there must be a better design available or the product is not unreasonably dangerous.

The evidence that the plaintiff must offer in order to prove the design defect is that there is a feasible alternative to the design that was used. The alternative design must be both technically and economically feasible of being used. Some jurisdictions speak of the alternative as being a practical alternative.

Defendants frequently respond to such evidence by showing that the designed that was used does not have a feasible alternative. The defendants will allege that the design was the state of the art at the time of manufacture.

As noted immediately above, one of the types of evidence that parties may use on this issue is customary design in the industry. The design that others are using is not conclusive on the case, but is evidence that the jury may consider in determining whether the design was unreasonably dangerous.

Of course, both plaintiffs and defendants will also offer substantial expert testimony on the issue of design. Plaintiffs will offer experts to talk about the alternatives that would have been available, while defendants will offer experts to talk about the state of the art of the industry.

D. Statutes and Regulations

In a basic course on tort law, the material usually covers the relationship between statutes and negligence. This topic comes under the broad heading of negligence per se. That doctrine finds similar use in products liability.

When the plaintiff is suing in negligence, the presence of a statute will have the usual negligence per se operation. Where the statute exists, it will set the duty for the defendant. The violation of that statute will be negligence per se

Strict liability cases are similar. There are examples where state or federal legislation dictates particular types of safety designs. Such statutes become important in strict liability cases. With most plaintiffs' cases, the violation of such a statute will lead to a finding that the product is in a defective condition unreasonably dangerous.

The more difficult issue arises when the product that is at issue complies with the statutorily mandated design. The plaintiff, for example, may sue in strict liability for an injury due to a product even though the product met the statute. In such cases, the statute is not conclusive. The jury may still find that the product was unreasonably dangerous even though it met the statutorily mandated design.

In short, it should be clear that the statutes act as a minimum. When the product fails to meet the statutory design, that product is unreasonably dangerous. When the product does meet the statutory design, the jury may still find for the plaintiff.

E. Subsequent Remedial Measures

Fed. R. Evid. 407 deals with a recurring problem in tort law that finds special emphasis in products liability cases. Once an accident occurs, someone may feel the need to repair the area or the instrumentality of the accident. In a products liability case, this may take the form of the manufacturer deciding to change the design of the product once they have been notified of a series of product failures. A person who is injured in that accident, may subsequently decide to bring an action for his or her injuries. If it was the defendant in that action that had made the repairs to the location or instrumentality of the injury or changed the design of a product that caused an injury, the plaintiff may want to offer evidence of those repairs in an effort to show that the defendant was probably "at fault" in the first instance.

The older cases in this area are best exemplified not by products liability cases but by railroad crossing accidents. In such cases, an automobile may have been trying to cross a railroad crossing when it was hit by a train. After the accident, the railroad company goes out to the crossing site and makes repairs. In making the repairs, the railroad company may upgrade the crossing; replace the warning devices with newer, brighter lights or more bells and signals. That company may even add a crossing gate where one did not previously exist.

The driver of the automobile then sues the railroad company for injuries suffered during the accident. During the course of the trial, the plaintiff would want to put on evidence of the repair and upgrades made to the crossing. The allegation would be that the evidence of repairs proves that the defendant was negligent in not improving the cross prior to the accident. Even before the federal rules of evidence, courts would routinely exclude such evidence. The courts had two bases for excluding the evidence.

The first reason for excluding the evidence was that the conduct of the defendant that occurred subsequent to the accident was not relevant to whether the defendant was negligent prior to the accident. The courts would reason that the defendant may have used all due care prior to the accident. After the accident occurred, the defendant, in the exercise of reasonable care may have realized the crossing could be made safer. This analysis would require the exclusion of the evidence since the issue was whether the defendant was negligent before the accident. In addition, even if there was some possible probative value for the evidence, it was outweighed by the real fear of unfair prejudice to the defendant.

The courts would routinely state a second ground for excluding the evidence. There is a public policy that encourages people to continue to upgrade and improve dangerous locations. The courts felt that if railroads, in a trial, would have to face the evidence that the company had improved the crossing, such companies would not make the improvements. The courts felt that by excluding the evidence, the future defendants would be encouraged to continue to make improvements.

The traditional rule, therefore, was simple. In a negligence case, evidence of a subsequent remedial measure could not be introduced into evidence to prove the negligence. The bases of the exclusion were twofold. The evidence was not relevant to negligence and public policy would encourage the exclusion of the evidence. The federal rules of evidence adopted this position. This same position, clearly articulated in rail road crossing cases, would also apply in products liability cases based in negligence.

Even before the adoption of the federal rules, there were exceptions to the rule. The current rule states these exceptions as, "This rule does not require the exclusion of evidence of subsequent measures when offered for another purpose, such as proving ownership, control, or feasibility of precautionary measures, if controverted or impeachment." Fed. R. Evid. 407. The application of these exceptions can also be seen in the railroad crossing cases. The hypothetical could arise in the same manner as stated above. The plaintiff was injured and the defendant railroad company had made repairs and upgrades to the crossing. In this example, however, when the defendant railroad company is sued, they deny that they owned or had control of the crossing. Their defense is not a denial of negligence, but a claim that the plaintiff has sued the wrong person or company. In such a case, the plaintiff could offer the evidence of the repairs and upgrades. The purpose of the evidence would be to show that the defendants either owned or controlled the crossing. The logic of such a relevance argument should be clear. The plaintiff would be claiming that the defendants must have owned or controlled the crossing since they fixed it. The evidence would be admitted for the purpose of proving ownership or control.

The rule also indicates one additional exceptional use of the evidence. If the evidence is offered for the purposes of impeaching a witness, it may be admitted.

As long as the cases dealt with the issue of negligence, the law seemed easy to apply. If the evidence was offered to prove negligence or wrongdoing, it was not admissible. If it was offered for one of the exceptional issues, it was admissible. As the federal courts began to face increased numbers of products liability cases which used strict liability, the rules became harder to apply.

In products liability cases, plaintiffs began to want to introduce evidence of subsequent improvements made to products. The hypothetical example is easy to explain here. The plaintiff would be injured by a product alleged to have been designed defectively. Between the time the plaintiff was injured and the time the case goes to trial, the manufacturer of the product begins to make it using a different and safer design. The plaintiff would want to introduce the evidence of the safer design in order to prove that the product was in a defective condition unreasonably dangerous at the time it left the manufacturer. Courts were split as to how to approach this problem.

Some courts would allow the evidence to be admissible. Those courts reasoned that the evidence in negligence cases had been excluded because it was not relevant to prove the failure to use reasonable care at an earlier time. In strict liability cases, however, the condition of the product and not the conduct of the parties is the issue. The evidence of subsequent re-design of the product would be admissible to show the condition of the product. It would help illustrate that it was possible to make a safer design. Since the conduct of the party was not an issue, and the condition of the product was the sole issue, the evidence was held by some to be admissible.

Other courts excluded the evidence. Those opinions seemed to focus more heavily on the public policy reasons for excluding the evidence. They reasoned that the purpose of the rule was to encourage possible defendants to make repairs and upgrades to dangerous instrumentalities. Those courts thought the same rule should apply to product manufacturers. It would be in the best interest of the public to encourage product manufacturers to continue to improve the safety of products. It was thought that manufacturers might avoid making upgrades if it was known that such evidence of upgrades could be used against the manufacturer. Using that logic, some courts excluded the evidence of subsequent remedial measures in strict liability cases.

In 1997, the issue regarding strict liability in products cases was resolved by an amendment to Fed. R. Evid. 407. Prior to that time, the rule had only excluded evidence of subsequent remedial measures when offered to prove "negligence or culpable conduct." In 1997, the rule was amended to exclude such evidence when offered to prove "negligence, culpable conduct, a defect in a product, a defect in a product's design, or a need for a warning or instruction." The intent of the amendment should be clear.

It is recognized that there are three types of defects which may give rise to strict liability in products cases. The plaintiff may allege a mis-manufacture, a mis-design, or a failure to warn. This amendment to the rule was intended to exclude evidence of subsequent remedial measures in all three types of cases. The language that excludes the evidence to prove a "defect in a product" would apply to mis-manufacture. The language that excludes the evidence when offered for a "defect in a product's design" would apply to mis-design. The language that excludes the evidence when offered for the "need for a warning or instruction" would apply to failure to warn. Although this appears to eliminate any questions, doubts as to the full use of this rule remain.

First, the most likely use of subsequent remedial measures would have been in design defect cases. The most common example of the problem is when a plaintiff is hurt and the manufacturer feels the need to redesign the product. The mis-manufacturer cases do not raise the issue. In those cases, the evidence is clear that the mis-manufactured product has a problem. Plaintiffs would rarely, if ever, need to resort to showing that the manufacturer changed anything. In addition, the failure to warn rarely raised the subsequent remedial measure rule. It has always been clear that manufacturers could make different warnings. The fact that they changed the warning after the fact is rarely used. Because of these realities, there was no great need to deal with mis-manufacture and failure to warn with this rule.

Second, the rule still leaves an exception that may apply. The rule indicates that the evidence might be admissible to prove "feasibility of precautionary measures." It is recognized that many design defect cases will focus on whether it was possible to design the product in a safer manner. If the defendant denies that a "feasible alternative" is available, but has, in fact, changed the design of the product to make it safer, that evidence may be admissible. The plaintiff would argue that the redesign of the product that occurred subsequent to the injury reflects the "feasibility of precautionary measures." It is interesting to note that some jurisdictions have stated that "feasible alternative" is a required element for the plaintiff to prove in a design defect case. It would seem that the evidence of subsequent remedial measures would always be admissible in such jurisdictions.

There are, however, other conflicting issues arising in tort law that may also have an impact on this evidence problem. In the late 1990's, the American Law Institute issued the final version of the Restatement (Third) of Products Liability. This restatement tends to speak of design defect cases in terms of negligence. The plaintiff must prove that the product was an unreasonable design in light of unreasonable risks. If jurisdictions move design defect cases back to negligence and away from strict liability, the amendment to rule 407 was unnecessary. The initial language of the rule that excluded the evidence where it was offered to prove negligence or culpable conduct would control.

Application of the rule, therefore, may leave a few, small issues in question. It is clear that use of the evidence to prove negligence is not permitted. It may be admissible to prove such things as ownership or control. It is also admissible if it is used to impeach a witness. The rule does state that the evidence is also not to be used to prove the three types of defects in a strict liability products case. The only real question is whether the exception for "feasibility of precautionary measures" will allow the evidence to be admitted in design defect cases. That will require the review by more federal courts in order for a final answer to be reached.

Proof Checkpoints

- The factors to determine if the science is valid in order to allow the introduction of expert testimony include, but are not limited to:

  - Whether the theory can be or has been tested;
  - Whether the theory has been subject to peer review;
  - Whether there is a known rate of error when the theory has been applied:
  - Whether there are standards and controls over the theory;
  - Whether the theory is generally accepted in the scientific community.

- Evidence of custom in a products liability case is admissible but not conclusive on the issues of negligence and strict liability.

- Evidence of feasible alternative will ordinarily be presented by plaintiffs and rebutted by defendants with evidence of state of the art in design defect cases.

- The presence of statutes will usually set a minimum in a products liability case.

- Evidence of subsequent remedial measures in design of products will not be admitted unless the issue of feasible alternative is raised.

Chapter 12

Defenses

Defenses Roadmap

- Understand the elements and application of contributory fault.
- Learn the rules concerning disclaimers and limitations on recovery in warranty.
- Analyze the issues associated with federal preemption.
- Understand the special character of government contractors.
- Distinguish statutes of limitations and statutes of repose.

The major factual circumstance that raises defense issues is the existence of some type of plaintiff's misconduct. That conduct may take many forms. It may be a clear misuse of the product or it may be a careless use of the product. Frequently, the initial observation of the misuse makes it appear to be a defense issue. Before covering those misuses as defense questions, however, a general overview should be noted. The same type of conduct, that being the misuse of a product, may be raised as a duty question or a causation question as well as a defense issue.

In covering the duty question, the material noted that the manufacturer is responsible for foreseeable misuses. One way that may be stated is that the manufacturer has a duty to design the product in light of foreseeable misuses. If, therefore, the question of misuse was to be raised as a duty issue, the analysis would have to be whether the manufacturer designed and manufactured the product in light of foreseeable misuses.

The misuse may also be raised as a causation issue. It may be argued that the product had a defect, but that the conduct of the misuse was an unforeseeable intervening cause. As such, it would be a supervening cause. By analyzing the misuse in this manner, it becomes a causation question.

Of course, the following material will discuss the presence of misuse as a defense. In that format, it would usually be seen as some type of comparative fault.

There is an obvious question as to how to decide when the misuse will take which of the above formats. The answer to that question is that the decision is up to the skill and arguments of the attorneys. The attorneys arguing the case will try to present the factual issues in the light most favorable to their clients. The plaintiff's and defendant's lawyers will attempt, in the initial pleadings and during the proof of the case, to cast the issue in either duty, causation, or defense as a method of showing the favorable side of the case.

That leaves the question of why would attorneys want one form over another. It is important to notice the difference in each of the forms that the issue can arise. Duty, for example is a question of law for which the plaintiff has the burden of proof. The defendant, therefore, would like for misuse to be a duty question. The plaintiff would have to prove the duty and the defendant could seek, by summary judgment, to have the judge rule on the issue without the case going to a jury. In addition, a ruling in favor of the defendant would completely defeat the plaintiff's case.

If the court chose not to call the issue a duty question, then the defendant would prefer that the issue be one of causation. Again, causation is a burden that the plaintiff must prove. It will go to the jury, but causation will completely defeat the plaintiff's case. A finding by the jury that the plaintiff's conduct was a supervening cause will result in a zero verdict.

The plaintiff, however, would like for the issue of misuse to be seen as a defense issue. As a defense issue, the defendant has the burden of proof and the results will be determined by the jury. In addition, the majority of states now have some form of comparative fault rather than contributory fault. This will mean that the plaintiff's judgment may be reduced, but it will not be completely barred.

As the following material is described, keep in mind that the role of the attorneys in the case is important. It will be the skill and arguments that convince the court as to which format the issue of plaintiff's misconduct should be considered.

A. Contributory Fault

Contributory fault on the part of the plaintiff has been recognized as a defense to negligence actions since the onset of that basis of liability. It also finds use in products liability actions, including in modern cases, strict liability. The current trend is to move away from use of that contributory fault as a complete bar to recovery and, instead, have the jury reduce the damages based upon the plaintiff's percentage of fault. The basic elements of contributory fault remain the same under both doctrines. The only difference is the application of the rules to the facts.

In order for the jury to be able to use the contributory fault of the plaintiff, the defendant has the burden of proving the issue. The defendant must show that the plaintiff failed to use reasonable care for his or her own safety. In addition, the defendant must show that the failure to use reasonable care was a cause of the injuries that the plaintiff suffered. This test is the traditional reasonable person of ordinary prudence under similar circumstances analysis. The jury will be asked to determine whether the plaintiff met that standard. (For a lesson contributory negligence, see CALI Lessons, Contributory Negligence and Last Clear Chance, http://www2.cali.org)

In applying that test to the products liability action based on negligence, the case will be decided as would any other negligence action. When the courts began to adopt strict liability, however, a difficult issue arose. The failure to use reasonable care on the part of the plaintiff may have arisen under a variety of circumstances.

The development of strict liability was designed to make sure that the consumer could rely upon the expertise of the manufacturer in producing a defect free product. The plaintiff should be under no duty to inspect new products in order to determine whether they are safe. Because of that underlying policy, the drafters of the Restatement (Second) of Torts §402A, comment n, suggested that the failure to find defects should not be a cause for defense. Since the plaintiff should be able to rely upon the manufacturer to produce a defect free product, even the negligent failure to find defects should not be a defense.

The simplest example of a strict liability claim, however, would be where the plaintiff was aware of the risk associated with the product and unreasonably encountered that risk. Notice how that circumstances difference from the one above. In the above example, the allegation would be that the plaintiff failed to find a defect. Since the plaintiff should have no duty to find a defect, the failure to find one is not a defense. Where the plaintiff is fully aware of the risk, however, and unreasonably encounters it, then drafters of the Restatement thought that could be used as a defense.

Imagine, for example, that the consumer purchases a new chain saw. If the chain saw has a hidden defect that causes the blade to come off and injure the plaintiff, it should not be a defense that the plaintiff failed to carefully inspect the new chain saw and find the defect. If, however, the saw works well, but the plaintiff negligently lets the moving blade touch his or her leg, then the carelessness of the plaintiff would be a defense. In the first example, the plaintiff merely failed to find a defect. In the second example, the plaintiff knew the risks and unreasonably brought the injury upon his or her self.

It should be noticed that the second type of circumstance that may be used as a defense appears similar to assumption of risk. Since it requires that the plaintiff to know of the risk and voluntarily encounter that risk, it could also be characterized as assumption of risk. It is important to note that it does require an unreasonable assumption of that risk.

In addition to unreasonable behavior, the plaintiff's conduct must also be a cause of the injury suffered. This element can routinely be met by showing that the injury that the plaintiff suffered was within the risk created by that plaintiff.

1. Contributory Negligence

As initially articulated the contributory fault on the part of the plaintiff was a complete bar to recover. At the time of adoption of Restatement (Second) of Torts § 402A, this was, in fact, the majority view in the United States. Currently, the view of jurisdictions has changed substantially. A vast majority of states apply some version of comparative fault. Such doctrine will reduce but not bar recovery.

When contributory negligence was a complete bar to recovery, courts also used the doctrine of last clear chance to alleviate some of the harshness of the complete bar to recovery. Where the plaintiff could prove that the defendant had the last chance to avoid the injury to the plaintiff, the plaintiff's damages could be recovered. Due to the nature of the doctrine of last clear chance it has little use in products liability case. It would be a rare instance where the plaintiff was at risk of injury with a product and the manufacturer or seller had some immediate chance to prevent that injury. Because of such circumstances, the doctrine of last clear chance is rarely seen in a products liability case.

2. Comparative Fault

Since the adoption of Restatement (Second) of Torts § 402A, the vast majority of states have moved from contributory negligence as a complete bar to recovery and to a form a comparative fault. Comparative fault will reduce, but not bar recovery. (For a lesson on comparative fault, see CALI Lessons, Comparative Fault, http://www2.cali.org)

The initial concern with the application of comparative fault to strict liability was a question of whether it should apply at all. Some jurisdictions were concerned that application of comparative fault to strict liability would be inconsistent with the policy that places a heavy burden on manufacturers to produce defect free products. Most courts agreed, however, that reducing the damages award to the plaintiff based upon the plaintiff's own degree of fault was not inconsistent with that policy.

There are two major types of comparative fault that states have adopted. States have adopted either pure or modified comparative fault. For those that have adopted modified comparative fault, there are two variations of that form.

Pure comparative fault is designed to award the plaintiff some damages which are reduced based upon the plaintiffs degree of fault. The operation of this doctrine applies regardless of the degree of plaintiff's fault. If, for example, the plaintiff was 10% at fault, then the plaintiff would recover 90% of the damages. Even if the plaintiff was 90% at fault, the plaintiff would recover 10% of the damages.

Modified comparative fault retains a feature of contributory negligence. The basic dividing line occurs when the plaintiff's fault exceeds 50%. For the modified comparative fault forms, the plaintiff recovers damages, less his or her own degree of fault, only when the plaintiff's fault is less that 50%. For example, if the plaintiff's fault was 10%, then the plaintiff would recover 90% of the damages. If, however, the plaintiff's fault was 90%, then the plaintiff would recover zero.

As noted above, there are two variations of modified comparative fault. The differences are expressed in the statutes. One form allows the plaintiff to recover some damages if the plaintiff's degree of fault is 50%. Plaintiff's recovery is barred only if the degree of fault exceeds 50%. In such a jurisdiction, for example, a finding that the plaintiff was 51% at fault would bar recovery. This type of modified comparative fault bars recovery when the plaintiff's fault is "greater than" the defendant's fault.

The second type of modified comparative fault may be referred to as "equal to or greater than" form. In this type of comparative fault, the plaintiff's recovery is barred if the plaintiff's fault is 50% or greater. If, for example, the plaintiff was found to be 50% at fault, the plaintiff would recover zero. The plaintiff could recover only if the plaintiff's fault was 49% or less.

B. Assumption of Risk

Assumption of risk was a traditional tort defense that was created at the time of the creation of negligence. The doctrine had two major elements. The defendant would have the burden of proving that the plaintiff knew and understood the risk and voluntarily encountered it. Such conduct would bar recovery

As noted earlier, with the adoption of Restatement (Second) of Torts § 402A, it appear that a form of assumption of risk would be an important consideration. The drafters thought that the failure to find defects should not be a defense, but a knowing, voluntary and unreasonable assumption of risk of the product should be a defense.

The adoption of comparative fault as the majority rule, however, has had an impact on assumption of risk. Courts have routinely stated that assumption of risk is abolished as a separate doctrine after the adoption of comparative fault. Although the doctrine has been abolished, the application of the particular kinds of facts is still found in products liability cases. Courts allow the introduction of evidence of where the plaintiff knew and voluntarily encountered risks. The jury is then allowed to use such evidence as part of the balance in determining the percentages of fault of the parties.

C. Disclaimers and Limitations of Remedies

Disclaimers and limitations of remedies are routinely used as methods to bar or limit the recovery that a plaintiff may seek in a products liability claim based on warranty. A full discussion of these defenses appears in Chapter 4, D. That material should be consulted for a full discussion of those defenses.

There are times that the defendant may seek to use a disclaimer or limitation as a method to limit recovery in tort for negligence or strict liability. Courts have been less likely to allow such use of disclaimers. The policy behind the tort recovery is to make sure that the manufacturer produces a defect free product. Courts feel that allowing the disclaimer of those remedies would defeat that purpose.

D. Misuse

The misuse of the product can be raised in a variety of ways. The opening section of this chapter, for example, fully notes that misuse of the product can be considered as a duty, causation, or defense issue. Those examples are illustrative of courts applying those facts in the traditional contributory fault framework.

Some jurisdictions have sought to make product misuse a separate defense. This may have been done by statute or court opinion. Even where the misuse remains a defense and complete bar to recovery, it is usually necessary to show that is was an unforeseeable misuse.

E. Federal Preemption

Federal preemption is an expanding field in the area of products liability. Manufacturers have found that state legislatures and courts may tend to be sympathetic to local consumers. The manufacturers have found better support by seeking federal protective legislation. The attempt is usually to get the federal government to pass laws limiting the available remedies to injured consumers.

It is clear that where the federal legislation is on point and consistent with the United States Constitution, then the federal legislation is superior. State case law and legislation cannot be inconsistent or superior to federal legislation. It is, therefore, important to understand when federal legislation is to be considered.

The courts have indicated how the federal legislation is to be considered. First, if the federal legislation expressly states that it is to preempt state law, then it does preempt that law. That is, of course, the easiest example of preemption.

Federal legislation may, however, be found to preempt state law by implication. The courts have identified two types of preemption by implication. Where the federal legislation is so broad as to appear to cover the field of issues in an area, it is implied that the legislation preemptions state law. In addition, where state law is inconsistent with federal legislation, the federal law preempts the state law.

F. Government Contractor

A substantial number of products are purchased by the federal government. Those products may ultimately cause injuries to federal employees or bystanders. When those injuries occur, the plaintiffs may seek to sue the manufacturer of the product in products liability. The courts have created a special defense for manufacturers who sold products under such contracts.

The government contract defense has been recognized to have three elements. Those elements are: (1) the government prepared reasonably precise specifications; (2) the product met the specifications; and (3) the manufacturer warned the government of any known defects in the product as designed.

The use of this defense does have some interesting applications. It has its greatest use where the government is directly involved in designing complex equipment. Military aircraft, for example, have been found to be covered by this doctrine. Where the government buys routine products for use, however, there is less likelihood that the doctrine will apply. One could imagine that the purchase of routine office supplies would not give rise to the doctrine.

G. Statutes of Limitations and Statutes of Repose

Legislatures have passed a series of statutes of limitations. Every type of civil action must be brought within a certain time period within which the action accrued or that action is barred. The idea of an action having been "accrued" usually means that all elements of the claim have arisen. For an action in tort, for example, there must have been a breach of the duty and an injury in order for the action to accrue. For a warranty claim, there must have been a breach of the warranty and an injury for the action to accrue. Statutes of limitation are state law issues and may differ among the states. Tort statutes of limitation, however, tend to be one or two years. Warranty statutes of limitations tend to be four or five years.

Statutes of repose differ from statutes of limitations. Statutes of limitation set a maximum time during which an action may be brought with that time period set by factors other than the accrual of the action. Federal or state legislation may, for example, require that certain products liability actions must be brought with 8 years of a products purchase or within 12 years of the products initial manufacture. Notice that the time to bring the action may run before the plaintiff is ever injured. The plaintiff may, therefore, lose the action by the statute of repose before the plaintiff ever had the action.

Defenses Checkpoints

- Plaintiff's conduct may be used as an issue of duty, causation or defense.
- Contributory negligence was once a complete bar to recovery.
- The majority rule of comparative fault now reduces but does not bar recovery of the plaintiff.
- Federal law may preemption state law where the preemption is:
  - Express; or
  - Implied by the federal law covering the field; or
  - Implied when state law is inconsistent with the federal law.
- Government contractors have a defense for products made for the government when:
  - There were reasonably precise government specifications; and
  - The product was made according to the specifications; and
  - The manufacturer warned of any known defects.
- Statutes of limitations require that actions are brought within a time period after the action has accrued.
- Statutes of repose bar the bringing of actions after a time period based upon some predetermined event.

Chapter 13

Damages

Damages Roadmap

- Distinguish the items of damages and the appropriate method of recovery for:
- Personal injury; and
- Property damage; and
- Economic losses.
- Understand the use of punitive damages in products liability.

The plaintiff's ultimate goal is to recover damages from the products liability litigation. The basic concept of damages is to compensate the injured party. This means that the law will try to place the plaintiff in the position, financially, that he or she would have been in had the injury not occurred.

In trying to recovery compensatory damages as a result of a product injury, the plaintiff will usually seek to recovery for several items. Those items include certain well recognized claims. The plaintiff may seek to recover for his or her own personal injuries. The plaintiff may also seek to recover for damage to any property other than the product itself. The plaintiff may seek to recover for other economic losses that occurred as a result of the product failure.

In addition to the compensatory damages, the plaintiff may also seek to recover punitive damages. Those damages would be intended to punish the defendant and are not based on attempts to compensate the injured party.

A. Personal Injury

Recovery of personal injury damages is one of the traditional forms of relief available in tort law. Being generally available in tort, it can be recovered in products liability actions based on negligence or strict liability. These personal injury losses are also recoverable under the warranty theories. It is obvious, therefore, that the personal injury losses make up the largest share of the damages in a products liability case. (For a lesson on personal injury damages, see CALI Lessons, Damages for Personal Injuries, http://www2.cali.org)

The personal injury losses may include a range of specific measures. The initial damages for medical bills and expenses are clearly recoverable. In addition, the cost of future medical treatment and care are also recoverable. Although it may appear to be an economic loss, the damages resulting from past lost wages or future lost wages are also considered part of personal injury damages.

Although the items described immediately above are typical for personal injury claims, additional items may also be recovered. Emotional pain and suffering are typically recoverable in products liability actions. This broad area may include a range of facts raised by plaintiffs. It may include the traditional pain and suffering, as well as just items as disfigurement, disability, or even, in some jurisdictions, fear of future diseases.

There are additional items that have traditionally been allowed in claims by plaintiffs which are also allowed for products liability. Claims for loss of consortium or loss of services of minor children are recoverable.

B. Property Damages

Damage to property, other than the product itself is recoverable in products liability claims. Those damages are recoverable whether the claim is based on negligence, strict liability or warranty.

The typical property damage claim can be imagined from a hypothetical set of facts. Imagine that the consumer purchases a small home appliance like a toaster. While using the toaster, the item catches on fire and ultimately burns the house down. The consumer would like to seek recovery for the house. This would be the type of "other property" clearly recoverable in products liability claims.

The measure of loss for such property damages claims will usually take a simple, traditional form. The courts will usually award damages based upon the difference between the value of the property before the injury and the value of the property after the injury. That difference will be the recoverable loss. For lessons covering damage to personal property see CALI Lessons, Fundamentals of Damages for Harm to Personal Property, http://www2.cali.org)

C. Economic Losses

Pure economic losses create something of a difficulty for products liability cases. The problem begins with the fact that there are, at least, two types of economic losses.

The first type may be those economic losses that occur because a product was defective. Imagine, for example, that a business buys a truck to make deliveries for that business. The truck is defective and must spend two weeks being repaired. During that two week period, the business loses money due to the absence of the truck. The loss of business would be a pure economic loss. Those losses would be recoverable under warranty claims.

The second type of economic loss would be the reduction in value of the product itself. Imagine, for example, that the business bought the truck under the warranty that the truck would hold 2 tons of material that the business needed to deliver. After using the truck for about a month, the business discovers that the truck will only hold about 1 ton of material. The truck is of reduced value to the business because of this difference. Clearly such losses are recoverable in warranty claims. The basis of the claim is that the product is not as warranty. The plaintiff must be able to recover the loss of the value of the product.

The product may also be of reduced value when it is defective and damages itself. Imagine, for example, that the truck mentioned above has a defective engine. The engine locks up and must be repaired. The damaged engine would also be viewed as a loss of value of the product. Those damages would be recoverable under the warranty claims.

The issue is more difficult when the plaintiff seeks to recover any of those economic losses under one of the tort remedies. The plaintiff may, for example, seek to recover the economic losses in negligence or strict liability.

The traditional rule of negligence law is that negligence may not be used to recover economic losses. That rule has been applied to product liability cases. The plaintiff may not use negligence to recover the economic losses mentioned above.

With the adoption of strict liability, the courts struggled to determine whether strict liability could be used to recover economic losses. It was determined that strict liability could not be used to recover such things as loss profits or other such economic losses. The difficult issue was whether strict liability could be used to recover for the reduced value of the product itself.

The Restatement (Second) of Torts § 402A mentions that damages may be rewarded for "physical harm ... caused ... to ... property." Plaintiffs, of course, argued that this phrase could be interpreted to include the reduced value to the product itself. Defendants claimed that the phrase only meant that damages for injury to "other property" could be recovered. Two early decisions seemed to frame the issue for the rest of the United States. In *Santor v. A & M Karagheusian, Inc.*, 44 N.J. 52, 207 A.2d 305 (1965), New Jersey allowed recovery for the loss of value of the product itself. In *Seely v. White Motor Co.*, 403 P.2d 145 (Cal. 1965), California denied such recovery. Almost every other state has had to address this issue and frequently cited both of those cases as methods of analysis to determine the outcome. The vast majority of states have adopted the *Seely* approach and deny the plaintiff's recovery for loss of value of the product itself under strict liability. A subsequent United States Supreme Court case, *East River Steamship Corp. v. Transamerica Delaval, Inc.*, 476 U.S. 858 (1986) has also followed the *Seely* logic.

The issue of economic losses points out one of the important reasons that plaintiffs in products liability actions find it necessary to use a variety of claims for relief. Where, for example, the economic losses, including the loss of value of the product itself, are high, warranty claims must be brought.

D. Punitive Damages

Punitive damages may also be sought by plaintiffs in products liability cases. The basis of the claim, however, becomes critical when such damages are sought. Punitive damages are intended to punish the wrongdoer and try to prevent such conduct from occurring in the future. Because of the purposes of punitive damages, the courts require something approaching intent on the part of the defendant before such damages may be awarded.

Because of the needed element of fault, defendants have argued that punitive damages are inconsistent with products liability claims. Where, for example, the plaintiff claims strict liability, the defendants have alleged that the plaintiff should not be able to recover the punitive damages.

Courts will not allow the plaintiff to recover punitive damages when the claim is based on strict liability alone. That same result is reached if the claim is based on negligence or warranty. There is nothing, however, inconsistent with a plaintiff alleging strict liability, negligence, warranty and then adding a claim of gross, willful, malicious or wanton behavior. If the plaintiff seeks punitive damages, claims based on strict liability, negligence or warranty will not support the punitive damages claim. The plaintiff must add the claims of intent, gross, willful, wanton or malicious. It is the addition of the higher degrees of fault that will support the punitive damages claim.

Damages Checkpoints

- Personal injury losses can be recovered in negligence, strict liability, and warranty.

- Property damage losses can be recovered in negligence, strict liability and warranty.

- Economic losses can only be recovered in warranty.

- Punitive damages may be recovered in products liability claims but the plaintiff must add allegation of fault behavior at a level higher than negligence.

Mastering Products Liability Checklist

The following reflects the topics covered in each chapter. A thorough understanding and knowledge of each of the items mentioned will be necessary for a good background in Products Liability.

Chapter 1 · History and Background to Products Liability
- ❏ The history and background of tort and warranty led to the current law on products liability.
- ❏ Negligence, strict liability, warranty and misrepresentation are the bases of the usual claims in products liability.

Chapter 2 · Negligence
- ❏ Negligence elements include duty, breach, injury and causation.
- ❏ Res ipsa loquitur is an inference that assists the plaintiff in proving breach.

Chapter 3 · Strict Liability in Tort
- ❏ Strict liability, and the elements of that claim were created in Restatement (Second) of Torts § 402A.
- ❏ "Defective condition unreasonably dangerous" is the critical and key phrase for understanding strict liability.

Chapter 4 · Warranty
- ❏ Warranty claims may include express warranties, implied warranties of merchantability and implied warranties of fitness for a particular purpose.

Chapter 5 · Misrepresentation
- ❏ Misrepresentation elements for products liability claims are the same as the traditional tort of misrepresentation.
- ❏ Misrepresentation claims for products liability may be based on negligence, strict liability or intent.

Chapter 6 · Parties

❑ The plaintiffs to a products liability claim based in tort are usually included in the phrase "user or consumer."

❑ The proper plaintiffs to warranty claims are defined in the Uniform Commercial Code.

❑ Special rules apply to the proper defendant. The issue may arise when plaintiffs have sought to sue:

❑ Component part manufacturers.

❑ Manufacturers.

❑ Wholesalers.

❑ Retailers.

❑ Used product dealers.

❑ Successor corporations.

❑ Endorsers.

Chapter 7 · Manufacture

❑ Actions based on mis-manufacturing of products are primarily proof of fact problems.

❑ Departure from design and malfunction are two ways of proving mis-manufacturing cases.

❑ Food and beverage cases have special issues associated with them.

Chapter 8 · Design

❑ Courts have created a series of different tests to determine when a design is in a defective condition unreasonably dangerous.

❑ Some design issues may be determined to be unavoidable unsafe.

Chapter 9 · Warning

❑ Warning cases appear to be based on negligence.

❑ Warnings will be analyzed by the courts to determine whether they are adequate.

Chapter 10 · Causation

❑ Cause in fact issues in products liability have been analyzed using the but for test and the substantial factor test.

❑ Because of the complexity of products liability cases, proximate cause raises a series of problems.

❑ Warning cases have a unique causation issue.

Chapter 11 · Additional Proof Problems

❑ Modern cases have a complex set of principles that govern the use of expert witnesses.

❏ Products liability cases raise special problems with the proof of custom, state of the art, feasible alternatives, statutes, and subsequent remedial measures.

Chapter 12 · Defenses

❏ Comparative fault is generally available for actions based on negligence or strict liability.

❏ Disclaimers and limitations of remedies are generally available for actions based on warranty.

❏ Federal preemption is a modern issue that arises in products liability cases.

❏ Government contracts provide a special defense in products liability cases.

❏ Statutes of limitations and statures of repose must be distinguished.

Chapter 13 · Damages

❏ Personal injury and property damages may be recovered in negligence, strict liability and warranty.

❏ Economic losses may be recovered in warranty.

❏ Punitive damages may be recovered if the plaintiff can prove a degree of fault higher than negligence.

Index